Synchronicity and Reunion

The Genetic Connection of Adoptees and Birthparents

Synchronicity and Reunion

The Genetic Connection of Adoptees and Birthparents

LaVonne Harper Stiffler

1992
FEA Publishing
Hobe Sound, Florida

SYNCHRONICITY AND REUNION:
The Genetic Connection of
  Adoptees and Birthparents

First edition, 1992

Copyright © 1992 by LaVonne Harper Stiffler
Motek Communications, Inc.

Published in the United States by
FEA Publishing
P. O. Box 1065
Hobe Sound, FL 33475
FAX 407-546-9379

All rights reserved. No part of this book may be
reproduced, in any form, without written permission
from the author, unless by a reviewer who wishes
to quote brief passages.

Includes bibliographical references pertaining to:
  1. Adoption—Psychological Aspects.
  2. Coincidence. 3. Parent and Child.
  4. Science—Philosophy.

ISBN 0-9634410-0-0 (pbk.)

Cover design by Bob Bell
Möbius graphics by Curtis Hale

Printed in the United States of America

ACKNOWLEDGMENTS

I am indebted to those who have become my colleagues during the course of this fascinating exploration, particularly the 70 participating families, representing countless more from the complex world of adoption, who shared their most profound personal experiences with me. My dissertation committee at Oxford Graduate School (USA), the staff of the Bodleian Library, and tutors in the Department for External Studies at Oxford, England, were there to help and to advise me that this is just a beginning. Many of the distinguished authors, researchers, and clinicians on whose material I relied have been generously kind to read, to suggest, and to encourage.

My appreciation also goes to my circle of enthusiastic personal friends, and to my family, to whom this book is dedicated: Robert, my steadfast husband, and our children: Lori Diane, whose life warms and enlightens our world; Gregory Alan, whose shining candle was transferred to heaven; and Lorelei, whose reunion brought a flame to dispel the shadows.

My gratitude, most of all, is for the Master Designer of unknown dimensions, who chooses to participate in ours, and who reminds me with a smile:

Now we see but a poor reflection as in a mirror; then we shall see face to face. Now I know in part; then I shall know fully, even as I am fully known. And now these three remain: faith, hope and love. But the greatest of these is love. (1 Corinthians 13:12-13, NIV)

LaVonne Harper Stiffler, D.Phil.

CONTENTS

INTRODUCTION:	*The Reunion Phenomenon*	1
1	UNION/LOSS/REUNION	7
2	WHAT'S THE CONNECTION?	11
3	CONNECTION BY PSYCHODYNAMICS OF SEPARATION AND LOSS *Impact on The Birth Family*	17
4	CONNECTION BY PSYCHODYNAMICS OF SEPARATION AND LOSS *Impact on the Adoptee*	33
5	CONNECTION BY SEARCH AND REUNION	39
6	CONNECTION BY COINCIDENCE	51
7	COINCIDENCE AS SYNCHRONICITY	61

8	CONNECTED BY A COSMIC DESIGNER?	71
9	CONNECTION BY NAMES	83
10	CONNECTION BY MEMORY	93
11	THE PSYCHIC CONNECTION	105
12	CONNECTED BY GENETIC ARCHITECTURE	119
13	CONNECTED BY FAMILY TIME	143
14	SIGNIFICANCE OF THE CONNECTION	151
15	SYNCHRONICITY'S IMPLICATIONS	167
APPENDIX:	*Support and Reunion Resources*	177
REFERENCES		179

INTRODUCTION
The Reunion Phenomenon

The final quarter of the twentieth century is witness to an unprecedented phenomenon: the reunion of tens of thousands of adult adoptees with their birthmothers and families of origin. Television, film, and print media have captured some of the tears and the euphoria of the primal reconnection. There are five to eight million adoptees in the United States (Van Why, 1977). As more of them become aware of the possibility of finding their roots, the number of reunions continues to multiply. A 1984 national survey conducted by a Washington, DC, organization, Kinship, estimated 500,000 adult adoptees were seeking or had found their birth families at that time (American Adoption Congress, 1990).

Reunions between adoptees and their birth families are usually the result of a long and arduous search process, particularly in the United States, where, at the present time, adoption records are sealed in all states except Alaska, Hawaii, and Kansas. Trends in open adoption, guardianship arrangements, and movement for legislative action to open records are a result of recent societal and psychological shifts toward the breaking of walls of secrecy, particularly as persons gain courage to speak of hidden trauma. As part of the fabric of socie adoption practice will eventually reflect moral, social, economic, and political change (Baran & Pannor, 1990a, 1990b).

In the meantime, in spite of barriers erected by decades of closed, secret adoption policy, **adoptees** give these reasons for seeking their genetic roots: They are trying to overcome a sense of existential alienation and loneliness; they have decided to begin letting go of denial; and they want to resolve loss and unfinished business (Small, 1987; Winkler, Brown, van Keppel, & Blanchard, 1988). The need for a historical sense of self is often triggered by significant life events such as the death of parents, divorce, medical emergency, or the birth of a baby (Sorosky, Baran, & Pannor, 1978).

Birthmothers who search for their missing children do so for the following reasons: They have gone through other life changes; they are affiliated with a support group; they want to know if their children are all right and alive; and they want to express love and answer questions (Silverman, Campbell, Patti, & Style, 1988). Through assurance that their children are alive and well, they alleviate guilt and restore self-esteem (Deykin, Campbell, & Patti, 1984). The motivation of searching **birthfathers** has a different component: They may want to retrieve or take back their children (Deykin, Patti, & Ryan, 1988).

After the search process (taking days, years, or a lifetime) reunion may be accomplished through a telephone call, a letter, or a face-to-face meeting. Even in those reunions that have elements of disappointment, rejection, or death, fantasy is replaced with reality, and the searcher can deal with the known actualities and move on. Adoptees report the bond to their birth families as a deep longing for kinship, generational lines, and connection with all humanity. Upon reunion, both adoptees and birthparents report "completion" in recognizing one's own blood identity, a life-course moment that seems crucial to their future development (Bertocci & Schechter, 1987; Modell, 1986).

Positive results in integration and identity were expressed in the reunion data of Pannor, Sorosky, and Baran (1974); Sorosky et al. (1978); Thompson, Stoneman, Webber, and Harrison (1978); and Triseliotis (1973). Silverman et al. (1988) found a definite correlation between what the searchers had hoped ... from the search, and the relationship they eventually found, in a ... irthparents and 114 adoptees. Ninety-eight percent of both searching and non-searching birthparents said they would again opt for reunion if given the chance to go back in time but not change any other factors.

Whether the adoptee or a birthparent has initiated the search, the majority are delighted to be found and report elation, catharsis, and ecstasy (Silverman & Patti, 1989). Leston Havens (1989), Professor of Psychiatry at Harvard Medical School, said he has "never seen such dramatic and rapid developments in human beings" as those that take place in the search process. Psychological growth, with its interactive components of conflict, ventilation of feelings, and behavioral change, takes place throughout the search, evolving from the time one decides to undertake it, through the obstacles encountered, and ultimately through completion and integration of what is learned and/or reunion (Martino, 1989).

After reunion, families begin to build relationships and to piece together the years that have intervened since their separation shortly after birth. They may discover mutual physical characteristics, creative talents, personality styles, distinctive mannerisms, and idiosyncrasies. Particularly surprising are the incidents of intuition and synchronicity that are common in post-reunion reports (Gediman & Brown, 1989; Rillera, 1991), suggesting a continuance of the prenatal bond, a psychic connection of the ruptured family system that transcends space and time .

Dreams of one's child in specific danger, naming a later baby by the unknown name of the first-born, vacationing in the same location, making identical purchases, and beginning to search at the same time are examples of the types of anecdotes I gathered from 70 reunited families for my doctoral research in behavioral science (Stiffler, 1991b). I was inspired by similar discoveries in my own family after our 1986 reunion with a daughter lost to adoption 32 years before. (Our personal incidents may be found as case number 36 throughout this book).

Such anecdotes of adoptee-birthparent coincidences appear in personal chronicles, support groups, and public media, but, until my naively begun exploration, they had received no concentrated attention. Parent-child intuition had been studied only in the normal context of offspring who were raised with their families (Eason, 1990; Schwarz, 1971, 1980). Psychiatrist Berthold E. Schwarz recorded hundreds of instances of telepathy in everyday life with his family, concluding that this means of communication is an important factor in the growth and development of children and their parents.

As recently as 15 years ago, stories such as these were not easily obtained, because birthmothers hid behind a self-imposed and societal secrecy, and adoptees felt the subjects of origins and reunion were taboo in their adoptive homes (Kirschner & Nagel, 1988; R. J. Lifton, 1976; Raynor, 1980; Triseliotis, 1973). In the safety of adoption support groups (see Appendix), which first arose in the mid-1970s, they began to express their needs, and reunions between adoptees and their birth families increased. They soon began to share stories of the unusual circumstances in timing and location that led them to each other, or their identical choices in occupation, grooming, or music.

I felt compelled to explore the nature of the extraordinary phenomena reported by so many people as humorous or uncanny coincidences, somehow marked in the mind and realized as significant at reunion, perhaps 20 or 40 years later. Do these experiences hint at a form of extrasensory communication, divine guidance, or a connecting genetic program far more intricate than yet unraveled by imaginative scientists? An exploration of these anomalistic (not following ordinary rules) phenomena seems important to a deeper understanding of the total union/loss/reunion experience of adoption-separated families. At the request of many who were curious to read the findings of my dissertation in a handier form, this book was hastily assembled. Perhaps a second edition will correct its inadequacies and expand its content. Input from readers is invited.

Because meaningful coincidences are personal and individual, they are not easily subject to scientific examination or statistical analysis. If a coincidence holds any meaning for others, it is because those persons share with the one to whom the coincidence occurred, some measure of significance in an otherwise neutral event. I chose not to debate what is or is not a synchronicity. **That which to an outsider might seem to be a trivial, chance incident may be called a synchronicity because it has subjective meaning for the one who experienced it.**

My sample was biased, because only those who had experienced meaningful coincidences were asked to submit stories. There is no way of knowing how many parents and children have discovered, post-reunion, that they are aware of no such coincidences. The effect of publishing only positive cases could convey the impression that anomalistic phenomena occur frequently in all adoption-separated families; this cannot be shown.

As it developed, the scope of my study included synchronicities between adoptees and birthfathers, and between other members of the birth and adoptive families. However, the essential focus began with the assumption of a mother-child bond known to begin prenatally.

What is, in fact, the nature of the mother-child bond? the father-child bond? Is a continuing psychic connection strictly genetic? One might explain similar hobbies, choice of a particular automobile, and the trait of claustrophobia, for example, on the basis of genetic research with twins reared apart. The memory of specific music may have originated prenatally. But what are the influences for vivid dreams, the naming of an imaginary playmate, or the strange drawing toward a particular location? Carl Jung (1958) believed that

> *Synchronicity takes the coincidence of events in space and time as meaning something more than mere chance, namely, a peculiar interdependence of objective events among themselves as well as with the subjective (psychic) states of the observer or observers.* (p. 592)

How does synchronicity function when an adoptee is separated from his or her birth family? Are reunions the result of answered prayer or unconscious longing for the missing part? The following chapters invite readers to feel the awe of reunited families, to join an eclectic overview of some possibilities, to ask their own questions, to tell their own stories, and to form their own answers to the enduring questions of **How? When? Where?** and **Why?**

For serious inquirers, there are an abundance of references and a few six-syllable words, to inspire turning to a dictionary or to other authors. More importantly, there is a treasury of simply worded anecdotes, that scientists might call "weak," but that speak directly and powerfully to the heart of anyone who has been involved in the real-life drama of **The Search**.

SYNCHRONICITY AND REUNION

> **NOTE:** All anecdotes throughout the text are from known, voluntary contributors. In some instances they have chosen to make changes in the names used. Because this is a cumulative story of many families who have experienced the union/loss/reunion experience of adoption, identification is limited to *case numbers* which follow the stories. *Letters* also describe the storyteller: f = female; m = male; p = (birth) parent; c = child; s = sibling; and o = other member of the birth or adoptive families. Example: (18fc).

The following words are interchangeable: birthmother = mother; birthfather = father; adoptee = child. When adoptive family members are mentioned, they are specified as such. The word *child* is used with honor and for simplicity, because in the English language the terms *adult adoptee, progeny, descendant,* and *offspring* are awkward in repeated use. Male pronouns are often used in the text for general reference to an adoptee, simply for clarity in reading material in which frequent female pronouns refer to a birthmother.

Categories have been assigned to the synchronicities, but they often overlap. The original narratives of participants were broken into paragraphs, with some having as many as eight classes, which include: names, search activity, places, vacation places, dates, courtship and marriage, birth, death, crises, intuition, dreams, memory, genetic architecture, religiosity, education, and occupations. Many involve coincidences between members of the extended adoptive and birth families.

1
Union/Loss/Reunion

It was a distorted time of muddied morality and good intentions, when two sins were whitewashed as solid walls of virtue in countless communities: The first sin was in maintaining the facade of a family's pride; the second and greater sin was in building an impenetrable barrier to separate forever a single mother from her newborn child.

Numb and frightened teenage parents Sarah and Alex lost their baby boy to a church adoption agency in 1960, and in a few months went in different directions. Through a path that included other children, spouses, and divorce, they made an unexpected reconnection. After writing, talking, and dating once again, they married in 1990 and resolved to break through every obstacle to find their son.

After a two-year search, they found him, a handsome young man named Steve by his adoptive parents, in a city of 500,000 people. They say their reunion was a remarkable thrill in itself, but that the surrounding circumstances leave them astonished: Steve and his wife had unknowingly purchased and were living in the very house where his paternal great-grandparents had raised a large family! A great-aunt still living next door had attended the christening celebration of Steve's new son, never imagining they were related.

Sarah, now unfrozen after 32 years of grief, her eyes glistening with tears of confident joy, told me: "I know God loves us. This is something much more than coincidence!"

That factual account is awesome. Who could begin to explain it? Is it more than an acausal synchronicity? What would lead Steve to buy that particular old house? Is it a paradoxical presumption to look for causality in genetic memory or biochemical makeup? The discovery of magnetite crystals in human brains, announced at the California Institute of Technology in May 1992 by Kirschvink, Kobayashi-Kirschvink, and Woodford (in press), may give one fascinating hint. Does a person with more magnetite have a better unconscious homing instinct, or at least a better sense of direction, than the average person? Magnetite has been known to be present in the tissues of certain migratory animals, ranging from bees to salmon, acting as a kind of biological compass permanently sensitive to the earth's geomagnetic fields.

Sun and light guide birds and hamsters, and an olfactory guidance system operates for bears. There may be no less a purposeful program for the human needs of nurturing and homing than those designed for the Arctic tern's 12,000-mile journey, or for the tiny eels that travel 3,500 miles from the Sargasso Sea near Bermuda to fresh-water rivers in Britain and Europe, then return to the Sargasso after three to eight years to spawn and die (Attenborough, 1990).

Might the human homing mechanism be tuned to persons as well as to geographic locations? An adoptee who is currently producing his own book on search and reunion wrote to me:

Many years ago I heard a theory about a tendency in some adoptees toward wanderlust (a strong impulse to travel). Why are some adoptees drawn to certain locales, often for no visible reason? Is there something there that pulls them to the place, even when they've never before been there and have no known connection to it? I don't know, but I can relate my own experiences with this: Florida--California--Alabama--Illinois. Why was I pulled to these states? Before I journeyed to each, I had no familial connections of which I was aware. Yet the pull was there like some distant magnet, slowly tugging at me until I succumbed and gave in.

Florida and California were surprises: My mother, sister, and maternal grandfather all resided in Florida, although I didn't know this until

> *I found them some 14 months after I started my first search. As it turned out, my aunt and her son—a first cousin—live in California. I can remember, clearly, feeling that there was something or someone waiting for me in each place. My adoptive mother used to think me slightly crazy when, as a youngster, I'd comment about either state. "Fantasy," she thought. How strange I should uncover family in both places! Or was this something I always knew but had suppressed, as psychologists speculate? (22mc)*

A female adoptee was equally surprised to learn that both she and her mother were living less than a two-hour drive apart, having moved to Arizona from Hawaii and New England before finding each other. "Why were we both in Arizona? Neither of us especially enjoyed the climate. We both feel that in the span of Hawaii to New England, Arizona must be a mid-point. Very strange!"

Was it magnetite, prenatal memory, or something entirely different that guided another adoptee who told me the following story? His unique personality shines through:

> *I was born and adopted in California, then raised in Pennsylvania. All my life, I felt out of place. I never really felt good about myself, because of a severe identity problem. I have always liked trucks and have collected Confederate flags and decals for years. I had a boat that I named "Dixie Darling," and I even have Confederate flags on my checks. Also, about a year before finding my family, I bought a personalized license plate that says "Southern" for my pickup truck.*
>
> *I never knew why I liked Southern things, until the social worker who was in charge of my search called to inform me that my birthparents were born and raised in **Georgia**! My mother went to California early in her pregnancy. I could have fainted. All I could do was keep saying, "I really am a **rebel**!" It was a dream come true. I am now at rest, knowing that it explains a lot about my thoughts, actions, likes, and dislikes. Now I know why I always felt like a Doberman at the Poodle Parade! (66mc)*

2
What's the Connection?

❖ *We know truth, not only by the reason, but also by the heart, and it is in this last way that we know first principles; and reason, which has no part in it, tries in vain to impugn them.* (Pascal, *Pensée* 282, 1660/1958, p. 79)

Are the technologically-focused "ways of knowing" of the Western world sufficient to consider the impact of mother-child separation and loss? Anthropologist Gregory Bateson (1988) found that the old, well-established ideas about human epistemology reflected an obsolete knowledge of physics and living things. "It was as if members of the species, man, were supposed to be totally unique and totally materialistic against the background of a living universe which was generalized (rather than unique) and spiritual (rather than materialistic)" (pp. 5-6).

Bateson's (1988) phrase for the symmetry of all life was "the pattern which connects" (p. 13), which he thought of primarily as a dance of interacting parts only secondarily held in place by physical and organismic limits. Schopenhauer (1891) visualized the pattern of causally determined sequences in parallel lives as the meridian lines on a globe, and acausal coincidences in two or more lives as the parallel circles. Pauli and Jung (1960, p. 514) used two lines intersecting in a cross diagram to balance dual perceptions of the same underlying reality: constant connection through effect (**causality**) at the left; inconstant connection through contingence, equivalence, or meaning (**synchronicity**) at the right; indestructible **energy** at the top; and the **space-time** continuum at the bottom.

MÖBIUS-CONNECTION PARADIGM

To add movement to these concepts, a simple Möbius band paradigm is helpful as an overall graphic representation of a mother-child connection that remains throughout the union/loss/reunion experience.

A plain strip represents the mother, and a shaded strip represents the newly conceived infant (Figure 1).

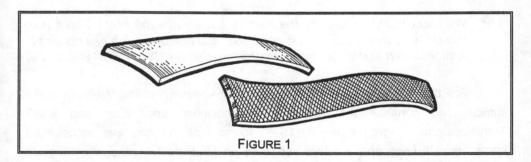

FIGURE 1

These two ribbons are glued together into a single *two-sided* band, symbolizing the symbiotic union of mother and child during the pre- and perinatal period (Figure 2).

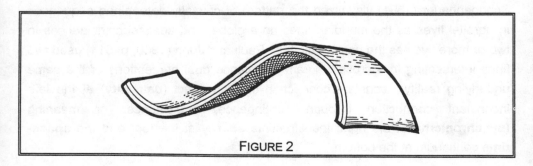

FIGURE 2

What's the Connection?

Separation by adoption is the point at which the strip is twisted 180º and connected by the mutual event of loss into a *one-sided* Möbius band (Figure 3).

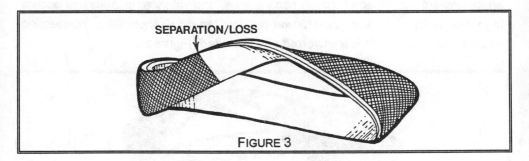
FIGURE 3

From that moment the arrows representing the life course of mother and child are seen moving away from each other in opposite directions (Figure 4); yet they remain somehow constantly connected through effect (**causality**).

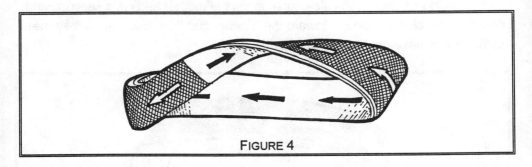
FIGURE 4

Each life is like a woven, flexible ribbon, occasionally crossing the expanse and touching the other at various points or intersections. It is then that an inconstant connection through contingence, equivalence, or meaning occurs (**synchronicity**). Like a short power-blast of **energy,** anomalous connecting information or behavior is transferred and recorded (Figure 5).

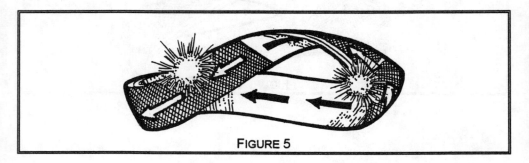
FIGURE 5

In the meantime, the life-course arrows of mother and child keep moving, now growing closer, pointing toward the other rather than away, until they meet at the **space-time** juncture of reunion (Figure 6).

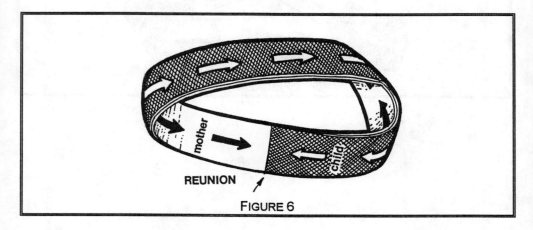
FIGURE 6

What's the Connection?

Through the strands of sociohistory and sociobiology in the personal reunion stories, a theme emerges that power, freedom, and energy come from casting away secrecy and becoming immersed more fully in truth than ever before. This burst of truth, of discovery, seems to take the reunited family through a black hole of "not knowing" to the other side, and beyond that to a perspective with a lighted overview of the entire Möbius tapestry. From here, the mother, child, and other family members recognize the various points of intersection, similarity, information, and synchronicity that occurred during their physical separation (Figure 7).

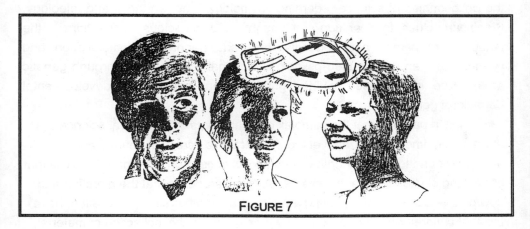

FIGURE 7

This paradigm is a visual and tactile representation of the words of poet T. S. Eliot:

> ❖ *We shall not cease from exploration*
> *And the end of all our exploring*
> *Will be to arrive where we started*
> *And know the place for the first time.*
> *Through the unknown, remembered gate*
> *When the last of earth left to discover*
> *Is that which was the beginning.*
> (1963, *Little Gidding*, V)

The chapters which follow are an inquisitive exploration of various ways in which birth families may be connected, and the ways in which those connections may contribute to synchronistic events. First, an introduction to the psychodynamics of separation and loss is presented. This includes the life-course impact of adoption on the birthmother, the birthfather, other members of the birth family, and the adoptee. Next, connection through search and reunion is explored, as missing information and relationships are filled in and coincidences discovered.

This connection by synchronicity is then examined through Jung's and Kammerer's ideas of acausal principles, and further opened for speculation in the philosophies of science regarding cosmology, time, systems, and teleology. Significant clues to cognition are sought in unconscious connections: the language of names and concepts; pre- and perinatal communication and memory; and an unexplained psychic link. Finally, connection through genetic architecture is examined in the light of recent research in developmental behavioral genetics.

It is a paradox that the complex compartments of behavioral science are at the same time specialized, yet highly interactive across ill-defined and arbitrary boundary lines. Another paradoxical dimension of human inquiry is that of seeking causes for acausal events. A third paradox is that the direction and flow of life-course arrows, moving away from each other since separation, have brought children and their parents together again. In this collection of material, the mixed pieces of these three puzzles are scanned and tentatively handled for possible matches.

3
Connection by Psychodynamics of Separation and Loss: Impact on the Birth Family

> ❖ *[A person may] be perfectly well able to live on, to be a man, as it seems, to occupy himself with temporal things, get married, beget children, win honor and esteem--and perhaps no one notices that in a deeper sense he lacks a self. About such a thing as that not much fuss is made in the world; for a self is a thing the world is least apt to inquire about. . . . The greatest danger, that of losing one's own self, may pass off as quietly as if it were nothing.* (Kierkegaard, *The Sickness unto Death*, 1941)

All parties in an adoption triangle have experienced a measure of loss, and because it has elements of hopelessness, it is sometimes felt and described as an existential loss of self (B. J. Lifton, 1988, 1992; Millen, Roll, & Backlund, 1986; Verrier, 1987). As Horney (1945) described a hopeless person, "He feels forever excluded from all that could make his life meaningful" (p. 183). In reality, **adoptive parents** have often lost the ability to have a biological child of their own; **adoptees** have lost identity and genealogy; and **birthparents** have lost not only an infant, but a preschooler, a teenager, an adult, and their grandchildren. It may not be until reunion that one is able to fully comprehend the deeper meaning of loss of self, finally recovering a new individuation and true self (Zinkin, 1987), and a wholeheartedness without pretense (Horney, 1945).

An examination of *The Adoption Bibliography* of the American Adoption Congress (Brinich, Bouchard, Speirs, & Brown, 1990), with 1,500 adoption-related materials, shows a preponderance of literature about adoptees' and adoptive parents' psychological problems and strategies for adjustment. It appears that only about five percent deal directly with birthparents' issues of loss, grief, and subsequent life development, and these are of recent origin. New Zealand researcher Joss Shawyer (1979) remarked after unsuccessfully looking through 20 books for background material on women who had surrendered children, "I began to wonder if adopted children had actually *had* mothers or whether they'd germinated on the window sills of social service departments" (p. 7). Since that time, more and more birthmothers are proclaiming their own stories, then going on in exponential leaps of personal growth to become attorneys, teachers, researchers, psychotherapists, and other helping professionals; their legacy in the literature is becoming more prominent.

Adoption research and literature of the past two decades has been criticized as having limited generalizability to the broader, nonclinical adoption population, because it has been drawn primarily from clinical samples or support groups already involved with issues of loss and reunion. Although there have been serious questions regarding methodological flaws, sampling bias, validity and reliability of measurements, and lack of theoretical context, A. B. Brodzinsky (1990) pointed out the valuable learnings from these past studies. The accumulation of anecdotal material from birthmothers, for example, has served to confirm previous clinical documentation of profound depression and grief.

Another problem is that the broader population of non-searching adoptees has not been studied separately; they have been included only as comparison groups in investigation of groups of searchers (Adelberg 1986; Aumend & Barrett, 1984; Reynolds, Eisnitz, Chiappise, & Walsh, 1976; Sobol & Cardiff, 1983). The adjustment of non-searching adoptees and birthparents is relatively unexamined. For the purposes of this book, those weaknesses in the literature are not a problem; only those parents and children who have gone through search and reunion have submitted anecdotes. Therefore, the following review of adoption's impact, although of limited generalizability, is likely to be representative of the contributing storytellers' experience.

Psychodynamics of Separation and Loss: Impact on the Birth Family

> Mothers and their children are linked in at least three ways: biologically during pregnancy, psychologically, and genetically. They shared the real space-time event of a unique birth experience. Fathers and other family members who are aware of separation from a child are linked psychologically and genetically. Siblings and others who have no conscious knowledge of a missing relative nevertheless have genetic kinship; for them, the psychological impact may not be felt until reunion.

Until the mid-1970s there was little information about birthparents' post-surrender experience and life-course development. The myth was assumed, after a single, post-placement interview, that in time these parents would put the crisis behind them and get on with their lives. Then adoption self-help and support groups began to appear: Concerned United Birthparents, Orphan Voyage, Adoptees Liberty Movement Association, and others (see Appendix). In these local and national organizations, which became forums for encouragement and discussion of shared experience, parents who had surrendered children for adoption found they were not alone. As they gained courage to share the depths of their secret grief, research studies followed, such as those initiated by Deykin et al. (1984), Millen and Roll (1985), Rynearson (1982), and Sorosky et al. (1978).

IMPACT ON THE BIRTHMOTHER [1]

From the mutual support groups (more than 400 in the United States alone) and the growing body of research, a profile of the birthmother as a hurting person can be drawn (although it cannot be generalized to all birthmothers): She has been numb since she first discovered she was pregnant (Silverman, 1981). Her pregnancy and delivery were characterized by feelings of isolation, alienation, fear, and inadequacy (Fonda, 1984). Under economic and social pressure, she felt powerless, with no choice other than relinquishment (Millen & Roll, 1985). From the time of the early postpartum separation, she has experienced her loss as an emptiness, a freezing, a wound that never stops bleeding, as arms eternally aching to hold the lost baby, or as a lim similar to that felt by families of soldiers missing in action (Anderson, 1987). Her experience of grief and mourning is inhibited and prolonged, because: The child actually exists somewhere; anger and bitterness toward others may be justified; and she has lost a sense of self (Millen et al., 1986).

Much psychic energy is spent keeping a secret of this magnitude and repressing her feelings, which may be exhibited in guilt, anger, an unconscious fear of sex, tenseness and uneasiness around children, a vague fear of discovery (Silverman, 1981), depression, social anxiety, agoraphobia, chemical dependence, eating disorders, or other anxiety/phobic states (Winkler et al., 1988). Her defenses are usually denial, fantasy, and repression (Rynearson, 1982).

She may be married to the birthfather (17%) and may never have had another child (36%) (Deykin et al., 1984). If she does have other children, her parenting practice is affected (81%); she may either feel she is unfit to be a mother, or be perfectionistic, possessive, and over-protective (Deykin et al., 1984; Winkler et al., 1988). She has never stopped loving the child with whom she bonded during pregnancy, and may report an apparent intuitive connection (Rillera, 1991; Schaefer, 1991). She worries about her child's welfare, not knowing if he or she is happy, healthy, or even alive (Anderson, 1987; Winkler & van Keppel, 1984). Her motherhood did not cease with the signing of surrender papers (Millen & Roll, 1985). She is haunted by the question, **Could that be my child?** when she passes an automobile from the state where she gave birth, when she watches Olympic competition, when she sees a new grave, or when she hears of tragedies involving adoptees like Lisa Steinberg, Karen Ann Quinlan, serial killer Son of Sam, homeless runaways, or teenagers in residential treatment facilities.

She is keenly desirous of reunion with her child: 82% in the study of Sorosky et al. (1978); and 96% as reported by Deykin et al. (1984). With a small sample of 50 Canadian birthmothers, 76.6% reported enthusiasm for contact with their children (Sachdev, 1989). An intermediary who has facilitated 900 reunions found that only 2% of the birthmothers refused contact (Sally File, interviewed in Branton & Snider, 1990).

Psychodynamics of Separation and Loss: Impact on the Birth Family

Birthmothers in therapy. A birthmother may appear to function well, often for years, then, for no apparent reason, find herself obsessed with the past and feeling a terrifying pain (Silverman, 1981). It is at this point that she may seek psychological or spiritual counsel, usually because of a triggering, life-course event, or for issues apparently unrelated to the loss of a child (Winkler et al., 1988).

In a study of the psychospiritual aspects of relinquishment, Barbara Dudrear (1991) found that about half of the reunited birthmothers who eventually sought professional counsel did so because of birthmother issues; the other half entered therapy for other life crises, such as divorce, but as time went on the trauma of relinquishment surfaced. In her sample of 64 reunited birthmothers, 70% had entered some kind of counseling, either individual (the majority) or group counseling. The average length of time since relinquishment before seeking help was 14.7 years. A woman who waited 25 years before telling anyone said she had denied her pain for so long because of the common advice to put it behind her and get on with her life.

The majority felt their time in therapy was well spent, but many expressed the opinion that helping professionals are not adequately trained to work with birthmothers. Dudrear found that, of the 64 women she studied, 49 had thought of committing suicide, and 14 had attempted it; all related it directly to the birthmother issue. One woman tried 12 times to kill herself; she stopped only when she found out search and reunion were possible.

Because a birthmother may never have told another person about her experience--not her mother, husband, children, best friend, or spiritual leader--a competent therapist will save much time by recognizing and addressing this core issue. Winkler et al. (1988) strongly recommended that any adequate counseling intake interview or questionnaire include the question: Have you had an adoption experience? Regardless of the number of years since relinquishment, telling the story can be profoundly painful, and a powerful process for both the client and the therapist.

Impact on sexuality. From clinical work, Sharon Kaplan (1989) reported a particular trauma for an adolescent who becomes pregnant in her early sexual experience. She may go through a post-traumatic stress reaction in later relationships, associating sex with the loss, shame, grief, and loss of control that accompanied relinquishment of her child. To lose the object of her most powerful instinctual attachment, her first-born, is a challenge to the foundation of a woman's desirousness, her natural libido being deprived of its object, according to Jungian analyst Edward Edinger (1987).

In a sample of 321 birthmothers studied by Deykin et al. (1984), those birthmothers who married reported that their earlier birth experience affected the marital interaction (71%), with problems in commitment, allegiance, and jealousy heightened during search. Birthparents who are married to each other seem to have a high risk of marital unhappiness and fragmentation in their relationship, but stay together because their shared bereavement is a stronger bond than commonality of spirit or interests (Deykin et al., 1984; Plomin, Defries, & Roberts, 1977).

Impact on spirituality. The relinquishment experience in its cultural-religious milieu has had a profound spiritual impact on birthmothers (Dudrear, 1991; Musser, 1982; Nave, 1989). Nave (1989) found that many birthmothers who went to their churches for advice and support during pregnancy were counseled in a manner they now consider antithetical to Christianity--shame-based and geared toward surrender. The results were feelings of demoralization, lowered self-esteem, and estrangement from the church. One woman reported, "The attitudes and actions of individuals and institutions representing the church are what caused me to leave and stay away for many years." Another said, "Adoption and the church are very much intertwined; they explained what adoption was and how, if I 'really' loved my baby, I wouldn't think of keeping him" (p. 2).

Part of the rage felt by birthmothers is that no one warned them of the severity of the depression that follows relinquishment (B. J. Lifton, 1988). Some were deceived by social workers who promised the baby would be placed with parents of a particular denomination; the truth was found to be otherwise after reunion. Upon learning that her surrendered son had killed himself, one mother went to her priest for consolation, who cruelly stated that sometimes children must suffer for the sins of the mother (Nave, 1989).

Psychodynamics of Separation and Loss: Impact on the Birth Family

In Dudrear's (1991) study of reunited birthmothers from a variety of religions, 38 of the 64 women reported having experienced a crisis of faith because of their adoption separation. This crisis was felt to be resolved by 32 of them after reunion, and their communication with God became direct, rather than through an intermediary or priest. The six who had not yet found resolution were in distress because of the discovery that their children had been physically and/or sexually abused.

Forgiveness is regarded by many reunited birthmothers as a major milestone in their spiritual growth, resulting from the search and reunion process. All but eight of Dudrear's 64 subjects had, in varying degrees, forgiven the persons they had blamed during the intervening years for separation from their children. Blame was attributed, in this order, to: the cultural system, herself, her family, the birthfather, and his family. Only a few blamed God. Today, after reunion, 54 of the 64 mothers described themselves as "a woman of faith and hope." The profound spiritual changes and long-term effects of reunion as a peak experience (Maslow, 1964) expressed by some reunited birthmothers seem to resemble those found by David Rosen (1973) in his study of survivors of suicidal jumps from San Francisco bridges, or by thanatologist Kenneth Ring (1984) in his study of near-death experiences.

During the years of separation, a birthmother with a strong religious faith may compensate for post-surrender hopelessness by becoming super-spiritual, submerging herself in church, synagogue, or community work, being judgmental of herself and others, and avowing a strong belief in the power of prayer. Yet, inside, she may have grave doubts and feel spiritually frozen, because her primary request to God, to know the whereabouts and welfare of her child, as mothers in biblical adoption accounts were privileged to do, has never been answered (Musser, 1982; Stiffler, 1991a).

If the day comes when such a mother is finally reunited with her child, it is typically described by her as a miracle of the highest order. It may have the numinous power of her first encounter with God, like a conversion experience. She reports a thawing; her self-worth and feelings of closeness to God are restored; and she develops a genuine compassion for other people as human beings. She may feel that the authentic self she acquired in her original dedication to God was lost at relinquishment and restored after reunion with her child, but only other birthmothers truly care or can understand the cycle of her grief.

Impact of grief. Studies of bereavement have progressed from a general understanding (Freud's "Mourning and Melancholia," 1917/1957) to a more specific comprehension of the unique types of loss and their differing manifestations. Bowlby (1980) asserted that loss is experienced differently according to the relationship of the mourner.

Anne B. Brodzinsky (1990), who has worked with her husband, David M. Brodzinsky, in adoption studies at Rutgers University, tracked the following variable stages in the grief of birthmothers: (a) **early grief**: shock and numbing; alarm and retreat; denial and disbelief (R. J. Lifton, l979; Parkes, 1972; Zisook & DeVaul, 1985); (b) **acute grief**: realization; protest, anger, and crying; expressions of outrage, guilt, and shame (Lindemann, 1944; Parkes, 1972); lethargy, cognitive confusion, and disorganization; yearning and pining; (R. J. Lifton, 1979; Parkes, 1972; Raphael, 1983; Volkan, 1984-1985); sadness and emptiness; repeated review of circumstances of the loss; searching; scanning groups of people for the lost one; returning to places where he previously could be found (Alexy, 1982; Bowlby, 1980; Parkes, 1972); feelings of powerlessness, despair, and low self-esteem (Bowlby, 1980).

In adaptive or normal grief, an end to the acute phase comes at a critical turning point: (c) **reorganization**: shift in cognitive and behavioral focus; increased self-esteem; personal control; reordering life in ways that do not include the lost individual (Lindemann, 1944; Parkes, 1972; Raphael, 1983; Schneider, 1984). To achieve the reorganization stage and an adequate adjustment, it is necessary to have an *opportunity* to grieve. For birthmothers, rituals and talking about the experience are important, ending once and for all the myth that things will be better if the baby is forgotten (A. B. Brodzinsky, 1990). For many birthmothers the reorganization process leads to *search and reunion*. This is different than in other losses, but it is still a reorganization of self to include the new relationships. As a result, there is movement into:

(d) **subsiding grief**: restoration and enhancement of self-esteem; subsiding of acute pain; caring for others and self; looking to the future; public or private animation of grief; self-help groups; public speaking and sharing (A. B. Brodzinsky, cited in Riben, 1988).

Butterfield and Scaturo (1989) suggested that the birthmother may be stuck in one aspect of her grief, or she may cycle between the stages throughout her life, in an ongoing, non-linear process of integration. She may not feel her grief initially, but will find it surfacing later in her life, perhaps at reunion or at the birth of a grandchild. She may not start grieving until as many as 40 years later, in a support group where she is free to talk, to open the closet and take out the grief piece by piece. "The grieving never stopped. It only went below my threshold of awareness for periods of time," said Schaefer (1991, p. 160).

The pathological nature of birthmothers' grief. Millen and Roll (1985) studied the ways in which the bereavement process was delayed or distorted in 20 birthmothers seen in psychotherapy for other presenting reasons. A chapter on their work, with the additional authorship of Backlund, is included in Rando's (1986) *Parental Loss of a Child*. They found these special problems of trauma which delay or confound a birthmother's grief, making it pathological:

The actual existence of the child somewhere interferes with her acceptance of finality. It may also complicate a desire to search, because reunion could be an imminent possibility, unlike the thought of ultimate reunion with a child lost through death. She has had other losses in addition to the loss of a child--perhaps her home or societal support. The working through of anger and guilt is impeded because of the secret, shameful nature of her experience, and the bitterness she feels toward others (e.g., social workers, parents, or society in general) may be justified.

The loss of self and the identification phenomena, as commonly felt after the death of a loved one, are complicated and confounded in adoption loss, because of the physical and emotional bond created during pregnancy. "I felt like pieces of a person, instead of a whole person," said one mother. Another said, "I sometimes feel I will never be complete" (Millen et al., 1986, pp. 264-266).

Summarizing the impact of their study and those of others, Millen et al. (1986) called for particular sensitivity to one whom they termed a "Solomon's Mother," from the biblical account of a mother who was willing to be separated from her child in order to spare his life (I Kings 3:16-28). In their recommendations and in their clinical practice, they have sought to honor the birthmother's continued emotional bond with her child, purposing never to deny, overlook, or denigrate it.

IMPACT ON THE BIRTHFATHER

Very little has been written about birthfathers' concerns. In the past, a young unmarried father was ignored and almost invisible, both at the time of relinquishment and in later life (Rogers, 1969). Research summarized by Kadushin (1980) indicated he was usually of the same age and socioeconomic background as the birthmother, and their relationship was of some duration preceding pregnancy. Clothier (1943) hypothesized that relinquishment has different meaning for a father, because fatherhood is not established in most men prior to delivery, but in fatherly activities that follow birth. In contrast, she said, motherhood is achieved in the months of gestation and parturition. This view may be challenged by the first study on the psychological reactions of relinquishing birthfathers (Deykin, Patti, & Ryan, 1988), and by personal anecdotes coming from groups such as the National Organization for Birthfathers and Adoption Reform (see Appendix).

In the groundbreaking survey of Deykin et al. (1988), 44% of the 125 fathers had at one time been married to the mothers of their surrendered children (25% currently so). At the time of the child's birth, most were young students or unemployed. About half of the sample (61) had some involvement in the adoption process; of these, 84% had agreed because it was in the best interest of the child, or because of their being unprepared for fatherhood.

Of the 64 who had not been included in the adoption decision, 89% felt that external pressure from physicians, lawyers, adoption agencies, or families had caused the separation. The resultant feelings of exclusion were reported to be long-lasting and pervasive. One father said, "I have never quite recovered from this experience. My father was upset and we never resolved it before he died. I feel guilty, selfish, sad, lost, confused, and upset whenever I think of her [the child]" (Deykin et al., 1988, p. 243). In that study, fathers who felt excluded from the adoption process and who later searched for their children, did so in order to retrieve or take them back, a motivation that differs from that reported by mothers. Mothers search to know if their children are alive and well, to express love, and to answer questions, according to the survey of Silverman et al. (1988).

> The fact that the search activity of birthfathers is highly correlated with thoughts of taking back the child should be noted by professionals in the adoption field. Such a finding may have considerable implications for how adoptions are handled at a time when birthfathers are affirming their identity through organized support groups and in the courts. (Deykin et al., 1988, p. 248)

Legal rights of fathers. Deykin et al. (1988) summarized that recent social change--brought about by the women's movement, a high divorce rate, and equal custody--has increased public perception of men as nurturers and not merely as the traditional providers and protectors (Bozett, 1985; Rotundo, 1985; Walters & Elam, 1985). Concurrently, Supreme Court decisions have affirmed constitutional protection for a single father's parental rights. The landmark case was *Stanley v. Illinois* (1972), which acknowledged for the first time that a birthfather has a legal claim to his child. Subsequent Supreme Court cases further expanded the parental rights of single fathers: *Quilloin v. Walcott* (1978); *Caban v. Mohammed* (1979); and *Lehr v. Robertson* (1983). States vary in interpretation of the laws. In California, when a birthmother surrenders a child for adoption, the birthfather's right to custody takes priority over that of prospective adoptive parents. He is judged to be the legal and therefore suitable parent. In Texas, a single father who has not legitimized his offspring by marriage or paternity affirmation has no separate legal standing as a parent when the mother surrenders the child (Deykin et al., 1988).

Life-course adjustment. Data from the study of Deykin et al. (1988) are inconclusive, but seem to suggest that the fact of having been a birthfather is not a predictor of the subsequent quality of marital functioning. Of 103 men who responded, 22% felt it had a negative impact, while 34% said it had a positive impact on their marriage; the rest reported mixed or no impact (Deykin et al., 1988). Men again differed from the birthmothers in the earlier study of 364 birthparents (Deykin et al., 1984), with relatively few stating that having been a birthfather had any impact on their parenting functions. In the sample, 23% had no further children. Willingness to identify themselves as birthfathers and to express concern for their children was highly correlated with their having a daughter rather than a son.

Fathers who were able to express helplessness and grief indicated that their pain was as deep as that of grieving birthmothers: "My worst, most painful mistake I have ever made. My life has been full and yet empty since the day my baby was placed for adoption. I would do anything to change that decision," said one. Another, after a successful search that healed some of the anguish, said, "My wife [the birthmother] and I have met our daughter after 25 years of separation and have had a close, loving relationship for the last two years. We are thankful for every day we have with her after a life of 25 years of suffering, loss, and grief" (Deykin et al., 1988, pp. 245-246).

Birthfathers in therapy. As in the broader scope of society, fewer men than women seek professional services to alleviate their emotional suffering. Men are outnumbered four or five to one in support groups for members of the adoption triangle. They may not be comfortable with self disclosure. There are also many birthfathers who were never made aware of the existence of their children, either because the birthmothers chose or were coerced not to tell them. It is urged that any counseling intake interview be designed to identify birthfathers, who may be grieving silently with unresolved issues (Winkler et al., 1988).

IMPACT ON THE EXTENDED FAMILY

Grandparents who are aware of the loss of their progeny are subject to the same cycle of stress as birthparents. Like families of MIA (missing in action) servicemen, their experience inherently encompasses Lazare's (1979) five social reasons for failure to grieve: uncertainty of the loss, lack of social support, socially unacceptable loss, social negation of the loss, and the assumption of the role of the strong one. A grandmother may originally have wanted to raise the baby herself, but was given no voice in the matter. If a grandfather was the one who urged his daughter or son to surrender an infant for adoption, there may be lingering grievances, regret, and guilt.

Psychodynamics of Separation and Loss: Impact on the Birth Family

With the freedom of societal openness that was nonexistent in an earlier generation, grandparents are now attending support groups and actively searching. For example, of 260 completed searches in a three-year period (1989-1991) by the Adoption and Family Reunion Center of the Musser Foundation, six were initiated by grandparents. Some grandparents, who were never informed of the pregnancy in the first place, are not aware of the existence of the child until a reunion takes place. They have a choice to be coldly cautious, or to become catalysts in the process of family integration and reconciliation. They may be shocked to receive a telephone call inviting them to an unexpected meeting, but, recognizing their own mortality, usually adjust with wisdom and unconditional love.

Siblings who are stunned to learn of a sister or brother they never knew existed must cope with shattered illusions: My parents are not what they seemed. Are there other secrets? Why was I kept and she given away? Guilt often follows this thought, as it does for one whose sibling has suffered an untimely death (Schumacher, 1984). As when parents idealize a dead child, and the remaining sibling feels burdened to measure up (Stephenson, 1986), resentment may flare at the flurry of attention given a glorified, reunited adoptee.

Sibling rivalry is a legendary, historical factor of human existence, in which children of any age vie for their parents' attention. It was a major dynamic 2,000 years ago, illustrated in the biblical parable of the lost son. The loyal, hard-working, stay-at-home son was understandably furious when an extravagant reunion feast, with music and dancing, was prepared for his loose-living, prodigal brother. The compassionate Galilean father replied, "My son, you are always with me, and everything I have is yours. But we had to celebrate and be glad, because this brother of yours was dead and is alive again; he was lost and is found" (Luke 15:31-32, NIV).

A sibling raised by his birthparents has just one set of parents, while a reunited adoptee has the attention of two or more. If birthparents are married to other spouses, there are additional stepparents and half siblings who come into the picture. Envy or grief may arise if one family has provided more material or educational advantages, and the cultural gap is broad. Often, though, siblings get along well because of their closeness in age, similar interests, and an immediate hereditary bond:

> [Although raised apart] both my sons played football, and they had the same jersey number. They had both sustained a football injury, dislocating a thumb. Both of them play golf and have a real aptitude for math and electronics. (65fp)

Some report becoming best friends, as indicated by reunited sisters:

> It was like we meshed. It amazes me. Now that we've become close, there is very definitely a feeling of oneness. When she gets depressed, I get depressed. It's like we're on the same wave length. (31fs)

Having grown up in an era more open to sexual honesty than that of their parents, young adults today feel free to acknowledge that they have gained, not lost, through a reunion. At a support group meeting of the Adoptee-Birthfamily Connection in Fort Lauderdale, Florida (April 7, 1991), I heard a young man whose family had recently been reunited with a lost brother express his delight and amazement at the changes in his mother:

> She has a new energy I could never explain. It's like she has had a blood transfusion. With 42 years of guilt lifted off her, she doesn't complain about **anything** now. We siblings are close too; it's like an adrenaline rush.

It is a great relief to the birthmother when siblings accept each other, for it expresses at the same time their acceptance and forgiveness of her. If they show jealousy, her allegiance is torn, and she may regretfully adjust by excluding the reunited child from the normal course of her daily life (B. J. Lifton, 1988). Many siblings do not understand the issues of loss which have pervaded the adoptee's life, and what to do about incompatibilities, annoyances, and new family boundaries.

Longitudinal studies of the post-reunion relationships of siblings have not been undertaken to date. It is unknown how their contact patterns and motivations will differ from the adult relationships of siblings raised together, as studied by Lee, Mancini, and Maxwell (1990); they found that emotional closeness, sibling responsibility expectations, and geographic proximity were most important in explaining dimensions of sibling interaction. They reflected internal states, cultural expectations, family norms, and opportunities. Kin contact was maintained regardless of affective feelings; the norm was actually a combination of obligation and affection.

According to previous research, sibling interaction was shown to be most frequent between sisters (Adams, 1968; Reiss, 1962) and between siblings close in age (Cicirelli, 1980). In twin studies, Rose and Kaprio (1988) found evidence that twins who engage in closer contact with each other in adulthood tend to be more similar in certain aspects than twins who have infrequent contact. Lykken, McGue, Bouchard, and Tellegen (1990) postulated that it is those very similarities which lead certain twins toward increased contact, rather than the contact's being the causal factor in their similarity.

In their study of the post-reunion experience of 30 reunited families, Gediman and Brown (1989) reported sibling relationships were affected by residential proximity, as well as by individual personalities, histories, and insecurities, and "ranged from extremely close to guarded and perfunctory . . . but there is only one case where the younger siblings' disinclination to accept the adoptee is proving to be a crisis for the birthmother" (p. 195).

NOTE
1. Material in this section was previously published by the author (1991) in the *Journal of Psychology and Christianity, 10*(3), 249-259: Adoption's Impact on Birthmothers: "Can a Mother Forget Her Child?" and is used by permission.

Connection by Psychodynamics of Separation and Loss: Impact on the Adoptee

In contrast to the paucity of psychological literature on the post-surrender life of birth families, there is a considerable body of material about the subsequent development of adoptees and their problems of adjustment with the adoptive families. The following studies are pertinent to an understanding of the impact of closed adoption practice on the psychosocial development of persons who have been separated from their families of origin:

Jernberg (1989) said in *Adoption Resources for Mental Health Professionals* that all adopted children, whether adopted at birth or at a later stage, have certain experiences in common: They have experienced a discontinuity between the physiological and emotional styles of the original mother and the later one, but have been expected to adapt with the least possible show of stress; and they have all experienced loss, rage, grief, and a serious threat to their self-esteem.

The psychosocial task of **infancy**, according to Erikson (1963, 1968), is the development of a basic sense of trust. Heightened parental anxiety or a mismatch between the parents' expectations and the baby's difficult behavior can lead to inconsistent caretaking and the promotion of a sense of insecurity or mistrust. The assumption of the duties of parenthood is a stressful process for most adults; it is especially complex for adoptive parents, who must also cope with issues of infertility, social attitudes, and timing of the adoption process (Kirk, 1964). After Reeves' (1971) analysis of the interactions between three adopted children who were his patients and their adoptive mothers, he suggested that they had come to each other as "aliens"; the fact that they had not shared the prenatal biological unity was a hindrance to what Winnicott (1956) called primary maternal preoccupation in the mother. In contrast, Plomin and DeFries (1985), in the Colorado Adoption Project, compared adopted and nonadopted infants at 12 and 24 months of age and found no important differences in development, temperament, and behavioral problems.

In the **preschool** period, children who have been told the events of their adoption in a loving emotional atmosphere show little adverse reaction, but exhibit a positive view of their adoptive status (Singer, D. M. Brodzinsky, & Braff, 1982), repeating with accuracy the story told by their parents. Any sense of loss grows along with their increase in cognitive ability, and typically appears in the **elementary** school years (D. M. Brodzinsky, 1984, 1987; D. M. Brodzinsky, Schechter, & A. B. Brodzinsky, 1986; D. M. Brodzinsky, Singer, & Braff, 1984). In that period of development, called by Piaget the concrete operational stage, children grow in cognitive and social-cognitive reasoning: reflecting, planning, analyzing, and logically approaching their world (Brown, Bransford, Ferrara, & Campione, 1983; Gelman & Baillargeon, 1983). Elementary children know that things and people have labels and names; they know the difference between birth and adoption; they realize there was a time when they were surrendered.

A sense of biological disconnection from unnamed, phantom parents often creates stress and confusion, unsettling any sense of permanence and security within the adoptive family (D. M. Brodzinsky et al., 1984; D. M. Brodzinsky et al., 1986). ***"Thus in the elementary school years, children view adoption not only in terms of family building, but also in terms of family loss"*** [emphasis his] (D. M. Brodzinsky, 1990, p. 13). Behavioral, emotional, and attitudinal changes appear, which D. M. Brodzinsky (1987) suggested are often a reflection of adoptees' process of adaptive grieving: anger, aggression, depression, uncommunicativeness, oppositional behavior, and self-image problems (Brinich, 1980; D. M. Brodzinsky, 1987, 1990; Nickman, 1985).

Identity formation. The primary theme of the **adolescent** developmental period, according to Erikson (1963, 1968), is a search for answers to the question, **Who am I?** For an adoptee, this also has the aspect of **Who could I have been?** Identity formation is a difficult and critical component in an adoptee's experience, because of the legal curtain that keeps information about his or her genealogy incomplete or unobtainable (Griffith, 1991; Midford, 1986, 1987; Sorosky, Baran, & Pannor, 1975; Stone, 1972; Winkler et al., 1988). Sants (1964) termed this experience "genealogical bewilderment."

D. M. Brodzinsky (1987) questioned whether those adoptees who have difficulty resolving the identity conflict may as a result also have difficulty resolving identity issues in such areas as religion, occupation, politics, interpersonal relations, intimacy, and sexuality. Brinich (1990) suggested that an adolescent adoptee's process of separation and identity formation is complicated by an unconscious choice whether to be barren but loving, like the adoptive parents, or to be promiscuous, fertile, and rejecting, like the fantasied birthparents.

Adoptees often describe themselves as a commodity or possession, abandoned or acquired for parents' purposes (Kirschner & Nagel, 1988). Adoptee and author, Betty Jean Lifton (1988), expressed the feeling of being an impotent creature without free will, the pawn of adults who forced an imposed reality:

> It is as if each Adoptee carries within him "the murdered self," which William James saw as the self one must not be. That self, the one born to another clan, with all the genetic pulls involved, must not be acknowledged. By being forced out of the natural flow of generational continuity, as others know it, it is as if one has been forced out of nature itself. (p. 64)

She pointed to the burden of leading a double life, haunted by a string of doubles: the self she might have become if raised by her birthparents; the self she might have become if chosen by other people; the child her adoptive parents might have produced, if fertile; or one they did have, who died. "The Adoptee carries this cast of characters around with him, hoping to find release through numbing, through psychoanalysis, through the journey back to the original self" (B. J. Lifton, 1988, p. 35).

Adoptees in therapy. In a national survey of child health in the United States (Zill, 1985), in which 348 nonrelated adoptees were included in a sample of 15,416 families, adoptees were more likely to have been treated by a psychologist or psychiatrist (13% vs. 5%; and 10% vs. 3% in the last year). Parents of adoptees rated their children lower on an academic class ranking score and higher on a behavioral problem index score in comparison to nonadoptees.

While one study (Marquis & Detweiler, 1985) reported more positive adjustment among adopted adolescents as compared with their nonadopted counterparts, the bulk of research indicates that adopted young people are referred for psychological treatment two to five times as often. As summarized by Grotevant and McRoy (1990), this finding has been replicated in Great Britain, Israel, Poland, Sweden, and the United States.

David Kirschner, clinician and director of a center for psychotherapy, testified in the New York case of a youth who was charged with the arson murder of his adoptive parents. It was from this testimony that the now controversial term, **adopted child syndrome**, was developed. As a consultant on capital cases, Kirschner found voluminous therapy reports which made no mention at all that a suspect was an adoptee, showing "the surprising tendency of many therapists to collude unwittingly with parents in minimizing the importance of adoption" (Kirschner & Nagel, 1988, p. 308). Kirschner made clear that while this syndrome is often seen clinically (he has seen more than 250 adoptees in intensive psychotherapy), he does not suggest that it is typical of adoptees in general, nor even that most adoptees exhibit it. In his opinion, adoption is a very positive alternative for many children, but it does present special challenges to parents and children. It may be an added, precipitating risk factor in families already predisposed to dysfunction.

Following is Kirschner's description of the symptoms, behaviors, and dynamics of the adopted child syndrome, as presented at the 1987 meeting of the American Adoption Congress in Boston. "Whatever one may wish to call it," he said, "it does not disappear":

> It is an antisocial pattern that may include: pathological lying; manipulativeness; shallowness of attachment; a lack of meaningful relationships; stealing; truancy; provocative, disruptive behavior--to parents, teachers, and other authority figures; promiscuity; academic underachievement or learning problems; fire setting; and increasingly serious antisocial behavior, frequently leading to court custody and trouble with the law. The pattern also often includes an extremely negative or extremely grandiose self-image, impulsiveness, low frustration tolerance, and an absence of normal guilt or anxiety.

Kirschner pointed out that the adopted child syndrome has similarities to the DSM-III diagnosis of conduct disorder, undersocialized, and it is probably most often labeled as such. However, what distinguishes the adopted child syndrome are the underlying dynamic issues related to feelings about adoption in both the child and the parent (Kirschner & Nagel, 1988). While not all problem behaviors are present in every case, they do tend to appear together in a large number of adopted children seen in treatment. Other researchers have come to similar conclusions, said Kirschner, and he cited: Goodman, Silberstein, and Mandel (1963); Menlove (1965); Offord, Aponte, and Cross (1969); Schechter, Carlson, Simmons, and Work (1964); and Simon and Senturia (1966). Their work has indicated that adoptees are overrepresented in psychotherapy and psychiatric treatment facilities, and that their symptoms and problems often fall into the pattern described (Kirschner & Nagel, 1988).

Adoptees in one long-term hospital treatment facility for chronically and severely disturbed adolescents were observed to typically exhibit dependency conflicts, severe separation anxiety, guilt, rage, and the projection of rage onto feared authority figures. Common defenses for their dependency and separation conflicts were splitting, denial, and projective identification. While the adoptees had similarities to nonadopted clients diagnosed as having personality disorders, in being more comfortable in a state of rage or opposition, a significant proportion of the adoptees did not finish the recommended course of treatment, and "they tend to have stronger needs to control the treatment, to have stronger distrust of the nurturing authority, and to persist in the use of projective identification even after many months of insight-oriented psychotherapy" (Goodrich, Fullerton, Yates, & Berman, 1990, p. 255).

Treating the adoptee as part of an interacting family system, rather than as a patient with intrapsychic pathology, is an alternate approach of brief solution-focused therapy based on the methods of Milton H. Erickson (deShazer, 1985; deShazer et al., 1986; Gilligan, 1987; O'Hanlon, 1987; Schaffer & Lindstrom, 1990). It has the advantage of not singling out the adoptee, who may already feel like an outsider in a non-genetically related family. The family system is considered to include not only the adoptive family, but also birth families, former foster families, social workers, and child care personnel. At the Center for Adoptive Families in New York City, the brief therapy team averages 6.0 sessions for families who adopted infants; 7.3 sessions for families who adopted older children; and 8.0 sessions for single-parent families who adopted at any age (Schaffer & Lindstrom, 1990).

Small (1987) said that adoptees are inclined to carry into adulthood the belief that their adoption is at the root of their problems. They become aware of boundaries or delineations between themselves and their families as they encounter major life events such as marriage, birth of a child, or death of a parent. This awareness is the beginning step in giving up denial of the existence of the birthparents and their shared heritage. Small outlined three stages in an adoptee's movement toward an integrated appraisal of himself in **adulthood**, the period in which the primary psychosocial task is the development of a capacity for intimacy:

1. **An emerging awareness and enlightenment**. The adoptee begins to understand that the need to know his genetic heritage is a matter of some urgency and part of his birthright.

2. **Giving up past enabling behaviors**. The adoptee stops trying to protect the adoptive parents from the realities of adoption, maintaining loyalty to the adoptive parents at the expense of his own needs, and allowing others to be in control of his destiny. He assesses and validates his long-denied feelings of anger and loss about his identity and adoptive status, and, as an ultimate act of reality testing, begins the process of searching.

3. **Integration**. At the end of the search, lifelong questions are finally answered, and there is a sense of completion, peace, accomplishment, and satisfaction. Fantasy is replaced by reality, which includes a unique, real genealogy and ancestry (Small, 1987; Winkler et al., 1988).

5
Connection by Search and Reunion

❖ *In all of us there is a hunger, marrow-deep, to know our heritage, to know who we are and where we have come from. Without this enriching knowledge there is a hollow yearning. No matter what our attainments in life, there is a vacuum, an emptiness, and a most disquieting loneliness.*
(Alex Haley)

SEARCH FOR MISSING INFORMATION

Like all mankind, adoptees share a universal felt need to remember and refer to the past, both individual and collective. Most people take history for granted as a heritage or force that produces a sense of continuity from the past to the future. Events are marked by time, place, and relationships. Adoptees, who in school study dates and events of other persons' lives, have no sense of where their own origins lie, no history of their own, and often report "coming from nowhere" as cause for "going nowhere" and aimlessness. In restless wanderings, they may seek companions of much lower social status than their adoptive parents, assuming a group identity to which they imagine their birthparents belong (Frisk, 1964).

The need for a genealogy is thought to be common to all adoptees, and not an indication of pathology or adoptive family dysfunction (Sorosky et al., 1975; Kirk, Jonassohn, & Fisch, 1966). In a comparison study of 27 searching and 17 non-searching adult adoptees, Adelberg (1986) found that the searchers' self-esteem was positively correlated to openness of communication about adoption within the adoptive family; and they did not exhibit more problematic psychological adjustment than the group of non-searchers. Among the searchers, 59% regarded their search as unrelated to their relationship with their adoptive parents, while 41% felt their search was in some degree related to dynamics within that relationship.

Psychiatrist Robert S. Andersen (1989), an adoptee, combined his clinical and personal experience to analyze the reasons adoptees search for their birth families in a report in *Child Welfare*: "The Nature of Adoptee Search: Adventure, Cure, or Growth?" He based his observations on the search activity of 100 people, and found three motivating perspectives. He stated that they may not be consciously chosen views, and most adoptees probably subscribe to all three simultaneously, but with varying degrees of emphasis:

I. **Search as adventure**. It is a simplistic, straightforward desire to pick up life where it was interrupted, and to share future experience with the birth family. Some who hold this view may not be prepared to find a mother who is rejecting or in an asylum, but most are quite willing to take their chances with the realities of life. This view of search as adventure is also a part of the following two more complicated approaches, both of which Andersen categorized as therapy.

When an adoptee says he feels incomplete as a person, and searches to resolve this issue, the search is seen as conceptually more intricate than simply adventure. It then has a therapeutic intent, with the goal of personal change, insight, or resolution. These models of **search as therapy**, according to Andersen (1989), are:

2. **The medical (deficiency) model**. Two things are presumed to be missing: a lack of information and a deficiency of experience. Cure is seen to occur when that deficiency is filled, as in taking of iron for anemia. The most significant aspects of this view are: (a) The adoptee needs to take something into himself; (b) this something is external; (c) the process is relatively passive; and (d) resolution is complete (i.e., cure).

3. **The psychological (trauma) model**. Essentially, adoptees experience something like a traumatic neurosis or post-traumatic stress disorder, presumably caused by dislocation and transplantation from biological to adoptive families. Treatment consists of acknowledging and responding to the trauma, then attempting to change a passive experience to an active mastery. It is thought that: (a) The adoptee suffers from a psychological trauma; (b) the

problem is internal; (c) treatment is an active process; and (d) resolution is incomplete. Reunion is seen not as an end, but a beginning step in a series of many toward growth and integration.

Andersen (1989) favors the psychological model as the most helpful, although adoptees typically exhibit some degree of all three models in their search for a cohesive identity. "There is, after all, information out there somewhere that is relevant to the adoptee's life, and since knowledge is power, it is hard to believe that this information would not be intrinsically useful" (p. 631).

Birthparents, who have also suffered from lack of information, do not know if their child is happy, healthy, or even alive. In traditional, closed adoption practice, they have no way of knowing if a social worker's promises were kept, and if they did the "best thing" for their child. The child has been denied complete information about his ancestry, siblings, medical history, and the reason for his abandonment. **The entire extended genetic family system has a void in information. Their formerly complete Gestalt has been broken.**

POST-REUNION RELATIONSHIPS

When a parent-child reunion occurs, the initial task is connection and repair of the broken Gestalt. It is a period of completion and order, when missing information enters all sensory modalities at once. Then follows the post-reunion period, in which the significant task is the development or limitation of a relationship. For many, a certain measure of "separation" remains, as they struggle to maintain a sense of their own space, suddenly frightened by the unfamiliar feeling of being so deeply connected (Rillera, 1987). In a 1981 organizational statistical study by TRIADOPTION, 90.8% of 533 reunited persons rated their reunions as favorable, and 9.2% as unfavorable (Rillera, 1991).

In their sensitive book, *BirthBond*, Gediman and Brown (1989) provided 30 case histories of birthmothers, all of whom attest to being somewhere between happy and ecstatic that they had a reunion, but express varying degrees of pleasure and pain in the post-reunion relationship:

1. **Extremely happy**. These women find almost nothing bitter or painful about it. They felt a loving connection from the beginning; adoptive parents and

the birthmother's family are supportive or geographically distant; the birthmother has reached a state of neutrality or equanimity about the birthfather; and she is capable of accepting her child as a person, in spite of any flaws he may have. She does not allow disappointments to serve as chronic irritants.

2. **Somewhat happy**. These mothers are either happy in spite of the problems, or find that problems somewhat reduce the feelings of happiness. They tend to focus on the value of the relationship, not the disappointments, which may include: intense grieving; uncovering details of the childhood which cause them to conclude they could have done better themselves; and adoptees' conflicts or lack of openness with adoptive parents.

3. **Mainly uncomfortable**. Those in this group experience pleasure and pain in about equal proportion but, unlike the others, emphasize the problems. The relationships with the most severe strain are those in which: The birthmother can't reach a state of acceptance about the relationship; there is a discrepancy between what each expects of the other; there is poor communication; and there are feelings of disappointment and not being in control of what is happening.

There seem to be two divisions in the post-reunion period, with the early years being more stressful than the later years. Five or more years may be occupied with the therapeutic work of solving relationship problems and completing unfinished business produced by the adoption experience (Gediman & Brown, 1989). Some experts, like veteran social worker and author Linda C. Burgess (1981, 1989), feel scars will always remain. "The whole business is *so* complex. Loss cannot be made up after years--just repaired, maybe" (L. C. Burgess, personal communication, April 19, 1990).

There is no acknowledged role for a birthparent in the American kinship system (Modell, 1986). Some families encounter sporadic or long-term rejection (Cissel, 1991; Rillera, 1991). Obviously, reunion between mother and child does not occur in a vacuum. Fathers, siblings, grandparents, and all extended adoptive and birth families are involved, with their own needs and boundaries. In my study, each of the three preceding satisfaction levels was implied in the collected stories, showing that experiences of synchronicity during separation were operative and meaningful in spite of rejection or final outcome.

Connection by Search and Reunion

SYNCHRONICITY IN SEARCH ACTIVITY

> ❖ One everlasting whisper day and night repeated--so:
> Something hidden. Go and find it.
> Go and look behind the ranges--
> Something lost behind the ranges.
> Lost and waiting for you. Go!
> (Rudyard Kipling, *The Explorer*)

Like the migratory and homing behaviors of animals, which have been known, admired, expected, yet mysterious to mankind of all generations, parent-child reunions have an element of awe. After their initial contact, families begin to talk about the intricacies of the search process, and many are astonished by the synchronicities of location and timing that led them to each other. In my initial study of 70 families, nine of them had intersection in location during search, and 23 had coincidences in the timing of their search.

Some of the more notable anecdotes are those of the 23 families who perceived as remarkable the timing of their search, part of an unusual correspondence of space, time, and circumstance that resulted in reunion. Two searching adoptees were drawn to timely encounters with judges who unexpectedly opened records for them; four persons were approached by strangers who offered surprising information. A mother and daughter began working at the same store within days of each other. Another mother reached her son just before his planned move to a distant country. Members of four families began to make inquiries in a search for one another at the same time (within days or weeks).

> *I became obsessed with finding my son in January of 1989, but did not act on it until September 1989. When I contacted the agency, I found out that my son had requested non-identifying information on **me** in January of 1989! I am still involved in searching for him and know I will find him eventually. I am also an adoptee who found my birthmother nine years ago. We have enjoyed a highly successful reunion--extended family included. My mother and her sister had made the decision to search for me the same year that I searched for them.* (12fpc)

SYNCHRONICITY AND REUNION

Before searching for my son, I accepted a job 700 miles away from where I had been living, (unknowingly) in the university system where he had just received a master's degree! Why at this particular time did I hunt for my son? It turned out he was shortly thereafter moving out of the country permanently for three or four years! When I got to the state I called him on the phone; we had a very long conversation. He wanted to see me, so we had breakfast together the next morning. We got along great. I only talked with him about 12 hours, and now I'm going to be corresponding with him. (49fp)

I am a birthmother. My daughter and I were separated in 1957; the reunion was in 1985. A strange coincidence that seems to never leave my mind is this: Twice I moved away from the state where she was born, and twice I moved back. The last move was to the city that has the Vital Statistics for the state. Something seemed to push me back in that direction. Things started to happen then, and within five years we had a reunion. (15fp)

When I found my mum two years ago in June, they had just built an extra room on their house, with a pull-out bed. It was the first summer in many years that Mum and my sisters had not gone to England. So I happened to jump in on the scene that first summer they decided to stay home, and to be the first person to stay in that room. It was as though my new room was there, all ready for me. I am now going to spend several weeks with her, because I am finding it really hard to put all of my energy into my marriage. I need time with my mum first; my husband is really supportive of it. It is amazing; we are so connected. I can pick up the phone before it rings, and she's on the other end! (70fc)

*I had been searching for my husband's birthmother for four years. I was getting nowhere, so I decided to put an ad in the paper in the town where he was born, asking for information, giving his birth name. I waited and waited and received no reply. In the meantime I wrote to two schools and received a package from one. In the enclosed photocopies was a picture of a girl with his same last name. The search assistant who had been trying to help us did a DMV check to see if this woman's birth date was the same as the date we had for the birthmother. We had a match! So we sat down to try to figure out how to contact her. Saturday morning I wrote a sample letter for my husband. When I went out to the mailbox **that day**, there was a letter from my husband's birthmother! She had read my ad in* the paper (placed months earlier), but she had been afraid to answer until this time. I believe God decided this was the time for it to happen, since everything fell into place in less than a week, after four years of trying. It was just such a coincidence! (55fo)

For several months I had seen talk shows on TV and read articles about reunions. Walking together one evening, my husband said, "Now that your adoptive parents are dead, don't you have any desire to find your birthmother?" I said, "No, her life has gone on. I have no desire to interfere in her life. I'm secure; I had wonderful parents, and you're a wonderful husband; the main adoption I'm excited about is being adopted into God's family." Exactly two weeks later, I got the phone call from my birthmother! So I can't say I was totally shocked or floored, because I really feel that the Lord had prepared me. But I was really surprised! I tried to call my husband at work, but he was in a meeting; I called a friend, and she wasn't home. Her husband, our pastor, was there, so I shared my news with him. Then I got emotional! (18fc)

In August 1979 I started my search at St. Catherine's House, the Register of Births, Deaths, and Marriages in London. (My birthmother was visiting London on holiday at that time with her two other children! She had not been to London for 10 years and wanted to go to St. Catherine's House to search the records but finally was unable to summon the courage to do this on her own, because she didn't want to tell a lie to the kids about where she was going.) I continued my search by contacting the Adoption Society in December 1979 and was told that my mother lived in the United States, was widowed, and had two children. The Society contacted her home town in Ireland and discovered from the parish priest that my grandparents were elderly and that my search might cause them distress. They indicated that I should wait a few years before resuming the search.
In June 1985 I went back to the Adoption Society, and they agreed to contact the parish priest again. They sent a letter and awaited a reply. In the meantime my half sister, who had been told of my existence by my mother at Christmas 1984, had started to search and wrote a letter to the Adoption Society in July 1985. The letter was forwarded to me and arrived on my birthday on July 12! A week earlier I had visited a church and lit a candle for my mother, the first time I had ever done this. (25fc)

...rs were drawn to opportune meetings with judges who ...usual practice and opened their files:

*I had been curious as to who I was, etc., but it took me years to get up the guts to start searching. I did not tell my adoptive parents I was looking (for fear it would hurt them), so it took me forever to do my search. They had always lied that my birthparents were killed in a car wreck. There was synchronicity in my search: Two years previously, my birthmother had inquired about finding me, but a private investigator told her it would take $1,000. She is very poor, so could not proceed. Timing was very critical in my search. There were certain things, if I had not done them **then**, I would not have succeeded. I went to [a distant state] to inquire at a time when my birth records were available **for viewing only**. Just after that, they were closed. At another point, I had been working through a certain judge who I knew would not release any more information, but I woke up one morning and said, "I've got to go back to the courthouse **today**." There was a different judge there, who opened the file for me!* (29fc)

I had made an attempt to find my mother by going to court, without success, and then put it off for a year. When an adoption group organized a meeting to protest against sealed records, I went along, ended up seeing the judge, and he gave me a new decision! (33fc)

In the following cases, synchronistic encounters with certain persons, often strangers, were keys in opening doors to ultimate reunion:

In July 1989 my wife was shopping in a local department store. She began writing her check for the amount of purchase, and an older woman in line behind her looked at the name on the check. This woman said, "Which Dillard family are you related to?" "My husband is Alan," my wife replied. The mystery woman then said, "Oh, I remember Alan; when he was born, he was very little. I remember when his parents, Rose and Samuel, got him." My wife replied, "What do you mean by 'got' him?" The woman said, "Why, when they adopted him." My wife was so stunned by this information about her husband, which was unknown to her, she did not think to ask who this older woman was and how she knew so much. ***This woman remains a mystery.***

46

Connection by Search and Reunion

My wife spent the next month wondering if I had kept this information from her, if I did not know, or if this woman knew what she was talking about. When she told me about the incident in the department store, I replied, "If it's true, it is news to me." The following day I went downtown to the government office where I could purchase a copy of my birth certificate and overheard people discussing amended birth certificates and sealed files. When I went to the counter, there was one lady talking to a young couple with a child. That evening I stopped by my mom's and told her what had happened at the department store. My mom said it was true, and she shared with me what she could remember about the story and circumstances. I told her about my visit earlier in the day to inquire about my birth certificate, and she began to describe the couple that stood in line ahead of me! My mom owns a travel agency and had delivered airline tickets to the woman I spoke with, 10 minutes before I arrived at the same building! As I thought how weird this coincidence was, I began to feel what had taken place was meant to happen. My search was completed in October 1990. I simply feel wonderful! (63mc)

I had been looking for my mother since I was about 12, but really searching after I got into my 20s. About four months before I found her, I was doing some exercises to try to tap into my memories, to see if I had at some time seen my mother's face, and so forth. Around that same time, one of my sisters, a nurse, who knew nothing about me, was into spiritism and tarot cards. She said that **someone** came up to her at the hospital where she works and told her that she had an older brother. So about the time that I was really zeroing in on them, they started looking for me; even my sister and my grandmother did. My mother had been searching all along, but secretly, because the sisters didn't know about me. (56mc)

I always knew I was adopted, but my identical twin sister did not, until she was pregnant with her oldest boy. One of her aunts said to her, "You never know, you might have twins, because you are a twin." My sister asked her, "What are you talking about?" The aunt said, "Oh, I said too much! I think you had better talk to your mother." She confronted her mother and father, and they said, "Yes, you were adopted." So that is how she found out she was adopted, and not only that, but that she had a twin. She started to search, and I did too, at about the same time. A priest discouraged me by saying it would not be likely to find someone after so many years. But I kept writing, until someone told me to contact a certain society. **My sister and I wrote there at the same time!** They said, "Wait a minute! They have to be the same twins!" We soon met, and found our mother a year later. (67fc)

> *We had **everything** on my mother: We had her Social Security number; we had her birth date; we ran a DMV check in 50 states; we ran credit checks; but we could **not** find her. Then it was almost like I was directed. I was guided by a force that was beyond me--to the woman who took me out of my birthmother's arms and put me into my adoptive mother's arms. What happened was, I ended up going back in my research and finding the company where she worked 30 years ago. Through a couple of contacts I was able to locate the friend of hers at that job--who had been the "middle-person" in this totally private adoption! I contacted her, and only through her was I able to find the link to my birthmother. It was symbolic: This woman separated us; and then she brought us back together, as though it was destined to happen that way. It was really strange. We were absolutely baffled. (5fc)*

The mother's story that follows is reminiscent of the type of coincidence often experienced by authors and researchers when key reference works fall into their hands at the most opportune time. Michael Shallis (1983) was looking up an obscure Czechoslovakian journal when the catalog index cards flipped of their own accord to the needed reference. He also mentioned that Colin Wilson had an experience when a book fell from a shelf, opened at the exact passage he was trying to recall.

Arthur Koestler talked of the "library angel," and quoted the report of Dame Rebecca West, who had a remarkable experience while searching in Chatham House for the account of a particular incident in the Nuremburg trials. The abstracts were catalogued under arbitrary headings in many shelves of volumes, and she had spent hours in fruitless search. She went to the librarian and said, "I can't find it; there's no clue." Then she touched one volume, carelessly glanced at it, and "it was not only the right volume, but I had opened it at the right page" (Hardy, Harvie, & Koestler, 1973, p. 173).

> *Twenty-four years ago I surrendered a daughter for adoption as a single birthmother. Recently, with the help of a support organization, I located her. I have yet to contact her, as I am seeking God's wisdom on the timing and the approach. This is what amazes me: Three weeks ago, I sent a check to a person who would try to locate the adoptive father; we knew his name but had no idea where the family had moved. Fifteen minutes after putting that letter in the mail, I stopped at the library, even though it was late in the afternoon. I **happened** to pass a row of*

directories and began to leaf through them for the name. The first book of white pages I picked up was a city in Texas. And there it was, the adoptive family's name! Also interesting is the fact that I had just visited that city several times recently; a friend had moved there, and now she is gathering information for me about my daughter! (46fp)

A chance tuning to a television program opened a window to joyful surprises:

When my son became 18 I started my search, and it took approximately three years. Since the birth and adoption took place in another state, I ran into a lot of dead ends. I tried signing with reunion registries across the country. One of the registries to which I sent information was run by the university where I subsequently located my son! However, it was not through the registry that I located him. One afternoon I happened to tune in the last few minutes of an Oprah Winfrey show; she had guests pertaining to adoption and reunions. Her announcement at the end was that if anybody wanted more information, to call the number given. I was put in touch with a search consultant, and within one month I had my son's name and a post office box number.

    I drove 350 miles to the area and fortunately obtained an address from a delivery man. I just wanted to see my son's house and circumstances, not to knock on the door. I got lost in the process, five miles from where I needed to be. So I stopped and asked a young man who was washing his car. He asked, "Who are you looking for?" I gave the family name, and he said, "I used to live over there. I played football with him." So out of all the possible people to ask, I hit the jackpot! Of all things, he went in the house and brought a yearbook out to the driveway, and I got my first look at my son from his high school yearbook. Not knowing who I was, of course, this friend gave me directions, said he had seen my son the previous weekend, and gave me all kinds of information. It was just like fate!

    Later, when I met my son at a pizza place in a distant city, on the pretense that I was an old family friend passing through town (and I was!), we talked about generic things. Adoption was not brought up, because I didn't know if he even knew he was an adoptee. Toward the end, he asked if I had children, and I brought out pictures. He would look at them, set them down, then look at them again as we talked. Finally he just looked over at me and said, "You're my mother, aren't you?" I said, "Yes, I am." He was shaking. He said, "Let's get out of here." We stepped out, and he gave me a big hug and said, "I'm so glad you found me." It has been wonderful. He's a great guy. (65fp)

6
Connection by Coincidence

❖ *Miracles do not happen in contradiction to nature, but only in contradiction to what we know of nature.*
(St. Augustine, *Concerning the Nature of Good*)

How likely is it that separated family members will find connection through a meaningful coincidence? Certainly all human beings have parallels in basic life patterns: We are born, have dwelling places, eat, play, sleep and dream, go to school, mate, work, worship, and die. There are bound to be occasional chance coincidences with people, events, and circumstances, even between unrelated lives, and most of these are never known.

Ruma Falk (1975, 1982) of the Hebrew University, whose speciality is probabilistic thinking, studied the surprisingness of coincidence stories and suggested people are amazed when faced with a coincidence, because they underestimate the total number of surprising possibilities, or the number of pairs that can be formed from a specific number of objects. For instance, the probability is slightly over half that at least two out of 23 randomly selected persons will have the same birthday (day and month). Another type of coincidence, having a friend who knows someone who knows someone you know, is also not as rare as one might suppose, because that set of people could comprise a group roughly half the population of the United States (Bernard & Killworth, 1979; Falk & MacGregor, 1983).

Coincidences may evoke surprise because of a largely unconscious cognitive bias which Falk (1982) called a "selection fallacy" (p. 24). When unusual events attract attention, they are singled out and observed as under a magnifying lens. There are only 365 days in a year; an adult probably has 50 significant events in a lifetime. It should not be surprising that meaningful dates coincide with those of other persons, unless they are the *same* event, according to Falk.

Zusne and Jones (1989) posited that even precognitive dreams can occur by chance, simply because they are comprised of the same components--a vast number, to be sure, but not limitless--that make up human life, and "the dream events and the real life events--are like segments from two series of digits that happen to match" (pp. 178-179).

Combs and Holland (1990) argued that coincidences are much more than the endless shuffling and reshuffling of random everyday happenings; the frequent and dramatic nature of meaningful coincidences belies a reductionistic interpretation. All occasions when coincidences do *not* occur are of interest to statisticians; but to persons who have experienced unique, numinous events, the comparison holds neither interest nor application.

In considering the effects of psychology and perception, Zusne and Jones (1989) claimed that **magical thinking** is partly or entirely involved in any explanation of anomalistic behavioral or experiential phenomena that seem to violate existing scientific principles. When information is lacking, there is a psychological state of cognitive motivation to remove the uncertainty. Magical thinking is universal and involves the belief that:

> *(a) Transfer of energy or information between physical systems may take place solely because of their similarity or contiguity in time and space, or that*
> *(b) one's thoughts, words, or actions can achieve specific physical effects in a manner not governed by the principles of ordinary transmission of energy or information.* (Zusne & Jones, 1989, p. 13)

How then may anecdotes of coincidence be properly studied? Some authors argue that statistics of probability are appropriate in a controlled laboratory situation or when dealing with large numbers of similar events, but they are inappropriate for unrepeatable, subjective, real-life experiences. "In dealing with unique events in hindsight there is no sensible or meaningful way of estimating their likelihood" said Shallis (1983, p. 136). Yet statistical mathematicians Persi Diaconis and Frederick Mosteller (1989) of Harvard find certain general- and special-purpose models useful and informative in some circumstances. They are working toward a general theory of coincidences and have suggested four principles that must be considered: hidden cause, psychology, multiple endpoints and the cost of "close," and the law of truly large numbers:

> *The more we work in this area, the more we feel that Kammerer and Jung are right. We are swimming in an ocean of coincidences. Our perception is that **nature** and we ourselves are creating these, sometimes causally, and also partly through perception and partly through objective accidental relationships.* (p. 860)

Diaconis and Mosteller (1989) have proposed the use of a critical incidence study, to distinguish between those coincidences that are genuinely moving because of personal importance, and those that are amusing but not life-affecting:

> *In a culture like ours based heavily on determinism and causation, we tend to look for causes, and we ask What is the synchronous force creating all of these coincidences? We could equally well be looking for the stimuli that are driving so many people to look for the synchronous force.* (p. 860)

What could be more genuinely moving or life-affecting than the unnatural separation of a mother from her baby? In that context, when coincidences are discovered to have occurred to bring them together again, the significance is phenomenal.

SYNCHRONICITY IN LOCATION

In 39 reunited families who told me they found meaning in the way their lives had intersected at certain locations or places: 26 were instances of ordinary residence, work, or migration; 13 were vacation spots; nine were related to search activity; and six involved persistent thought of a certain place. One mother had unknowingly spent an annual Columbus Day weekend in the same motel as her daughter. Another adoptee for nine years chose to spend her vacations in a small, remote area where several generations of her birth family had property.

The following words were used by some to describe what they believed to be an extraordinary drawing toward particular locations:

> ***pull, distinct energy, like a distant magnet, strong connection, mid-point,*** and ***our paths crossed.***

Does this information begin to answer **Where?** and **How?**

> *When I surrendered my son, he went to Connecticut. Now he's in Florida and has been there for most of his growing up, as far as I can tell. My family has very strong connections to Florida, and at one time I went to the town where he lived. That was an area my grandparents were very attached to. (10fp)*

> *I was born in Hawaii but grew up in New England. I went to college for one year in Utah, then transferred to the University of Arizona. My mother was born in Mississippi and raised in Florida. I was born while she was attending the University of Hawaii. When I found her, she was living in Phoenix, Arizona, less than a two-hour drive from me in Tucson. Why were we both in Arizona? Neither of us especially enjoyed the climate. We both feel that in the span of Hawaii to New England, Arizona must be a mid-point. Very strange. (12fc)*

> *At one time I worked just three blocks away from my son. (3fp)*

It was so unusual to find that [in a large metropolitan area] for nearly three years I had been living just three blocks away from my mother, during the time of my search. It was a neighborhood where my husband grew up and had lived for 18 years. My mother had been there for nine years. Beyond that, we worked together in the same store for six months before we discovered we were mother and daughter. (64fc)

For 13 years my daughter and I were living within 50 miles of each other. This we found out in 1985. I had started the search in 1980. My daughter had tried to find me by writing the agency and was unsuccessful. Our minds were strong for a reunion. (15fp)

I met my birthmother when I was 12, and I'm 26 now. When I did meet her, she was living, and had been for several years, in the same trailer park as my adoptive uncle. She was only a couple of rows away, and I never knew it. (17fc)

My birth family moved in 1969 to a house in the same suburb just a block away from where I grew up. My younger brother and I went to the same junior school, but a year apart. My birthmother had attended sports days and puppetry shows at the school while I was there, aged 9 to 12. (19fc)

When I was in high school, I went (90 miles from home) to a girls' boarding school for two years, right across the street from the hospital where (I later learned) I was born. I went there for my doctors' appointments, and would go up to look at the babies in the nursery before I went back to school! (44fc)

My son's adoptive parents at one time had lived on the street where he was conceived. This is a very short street, and it's a big city; it's not a small town. (49fp)

My mother and my half brother and sister (from the United States) visited me in England in September 1985. I had just moved. Six months earlier I had lived in a little flat in Maresfield Gardens, Hampstead. My mother asked me to take her to Maresfield Gardens--to a little chapel where she had married the father of my half siblings in 1961! (25fc)

A father shared an account of synchronicity between his known son and the adoptive sister of a daughter he had surrendered years before:

*My son had been suffering from deep depression for quite some time and had just been hospitalized for almost a year. Then, at the age of 13, he entered a teenagers' house in an after-care facility located close to the high school he was attending. At the time there were only **three** other teenagers in residence, girls, one of whom was in the same school and grade as my son. A few months later I took on the volunteer job of locating lost parents for adoptees, and it struck me that I could use the skills I had developed to locate the family who had adopted my own daughter. This turned out to be a fairly simple thing to do, and I located the family, their names, and address.*

*The following day while returning my son to his house after an outing, I told him I had located his half sister, whose surname was now _____. He said, "That's strange—one of the girls living with me is named _____." We soon discovered she was indeed the adoptive sister of my lost daughter, attended the same school as my son, and that she had moved into the residence prior to him. Before that they had been in the same children's psychiatric hospital. **What is the probability that this would occur in a city of a million people?** Interesting, don't you think?* (8mp)

The next two adoptees experienced an intuitive fine-tuning in location as they completed their search:

When I finally met my birthmother, it was planned for a large shopping mall in North Jersey. I happened to park next to her car! It was uncharacteristic for me to park where I did, and I was tempted to move closer to the door, but yet I stayed there. (34fc)

Search itself was uncanny. Nearing the town where I was born, I felt a pull, a distinct energy. As we traveled the town, I began to feel "hot and cold." My companion at first was skeptical, but she soon began to trust my intuition. We camped where my family always went swimming as children. We parked in a vacant lot where my grandfather once owned a store. (48fc)

VACATION PLACES

Especially surprising to some reunited families is uncovering the fact that they have chosen to vacation in the same place. It may have been the choice of the adoptive family when the child was young, or the choice of the adult adoptee in later life. Are vacation spots selected in a special state of consciousness?

> *As a child living in California, I used to say that I wanted to go to the Florida Keys. That was where my birth family went each summer! When I was 33, they took me there too. (36fc)*

> *All my life I have been drawn to certain things and places (I find out now) my mother was also, or my sister. There is a small town here that I experience "strange vibes" in. I found out my mother was living there at the time of my birth. Also I traveled to South Australia in 1979 and was taken by an adoptive uncle (unknowingly) to the very places my mother and father were living around the time of my conception. I could not concentrate during my visit there for four weeks. I have now found out my birth uncles and cousins lived there then and are still there. (30fc)*

> *Our favorite vacation spot is Gatlinburg, Tennessee, even though I travel from Alabama and my mother travels from South Carolina. (4fc)*

> *I recently located my sister's daughter, who was given up for adoption at birth. We discovered a strange coincidence: She has been spending her vacations for the last nine years at a small, out-of-the-way place on the Cape, using a friend's guest house. My grandfather and grandmother purchased property at this same place many years ago, and we grew up spending our summers there. My parents built a house there, as did uncles and cousins. (9fo)*

> *My sister and I were both in Colorado in the summer of 1975. I had run away from home, and I have no idea why I ended up there. It just kind of pulled me. My sister was there on her honeymoon; we were within 20 miles of each other. (31fs)*

Synchronicity and Reunion

My daughter vacations in the same town where I attended school. (6fp)

In 1971 my husband and I went to a town at the other end of the state for a getaway weekend. Why we went there, I'll never know; there's really nothing there. What I didn't know was that my son and his adoptive family had moved there; they were living there at the time. (65fp)

When I was 10 or 11 I was sent away to a girls' camp in Vermont. I later learned my birthmother had attended a retreat there at a different time. (18fc)

I was amazed to find out that my family passed by my birthmother's house every summer for 18 years to get to our cottage at a lake only a few miles from her house. She and her family also used the same lake for fishing, from 1945 to 1965. (7fc)

When I met my birthfather, we talked of certain things we've done and places we have gone in our lives. There is a very small town in New Hampshire that has an annual Fourth of July mayoral-type festival. It turns into a big joke, and everybody laughs and has a good time. We both had attended that yearly for many, many years without knowing, of course, that I was there and he was there! I was brought up in Massachusetts, but we had a summer place in New Hampshire only a mile away from where this took place. Until I became a teenager my parents took me, but then it was my choice. As an adult I have also attended, at least between 10 and 15 years. My birthfather had to come 14 miles from his home to attend. (23fc)

My daughter and her adoptive father came to visit me in 1985. We all stopped in Bennington, Vermont, and I mentioned it was my "old stomping ground." Her father said that during Columbus Day weekend, he used to take the children to Vermont, and they stayed at the New Englander Motel. I used to go there for that weekend too, and stayed with my mother in that motel. It is very possible our paths crossed while we were there. For all I know, my daughter could have been in the next room! (54fp)

Connection by Coincidence

My mother and I always loved traveling and learning other languages. We had both been in Italy and the same part of northern France. (53fc)

My birthmum and I just kind of skipped along, missing each other by a few years. We had both been skiing at the same place in Austria. I thought I had the name wrong all these years, because I never met anyone else who knew of it. She said, "That's where I went skiing too!" Then she spent time in Amsterdam; I have been there three or four times. She ended up in New York, and I in California.

After we found each other, two months before she was to visit me, I booked a hotel in La Jolla for a brief getaway for us. I don't know why I did this; I had never stayed there before. In between, I found my birthfather and learned that my half brother lives in La Jolla! I had also unknowingly connected with this brother in another way: I had never before walked into a gym that was under construction. My husband and I watched one being built and thought it was wonderful. We joined it. Of all the gyms in Los Angeles, this one was designed by my half brother! It was really bizarre. (70fc)

7
Coincidence as Synchronicity

It was Carl Jung (1960) who gave psychological vocabulary the word *synchronicity*, which is now used by many as a general synonym for coincidence. He defined it as "the simultaneous occurrence of two meaningfully but not causally connected events" (p. 441) or "a coincidence in time of two or more causally unrelated events which have the same or similar meaning" (p. 511). His exploration of precognitive dreams was just one indication that his terminology of *simultaneity* was misleading; he sidestepped this time paradox by saying that *the unconscious mind functions outside the physical framework of space-time*. He explained that precognitive experiences are "evidently not *synchronous* but are *synchronistic* since they are experienced as psychic images *in the present* as though the objective event already existed" (p. 445).

Jung, like Freud, was an important shaper of depth psychology in particular and twentieth-century transdisciplinary thought in general. His major writing on synchronicity, to "open up a very obscure field which is philosophically of greatest importance" was first published when he was in his mid-70s: "Synchronicity: An Acausal Connecting Principle." He had collaborated in this speculative, universal schema with the eminent physicist Wolfgang Pauli, whose paper, "The Influence of Archetypal Ideas on the Scientific Theories of Kepler," appeared in the same German volume: *Naturerklarung und Psyche* [The Interpretation of Nature and the Psyche] (1952/1955).

Jung (1960) described three types of synchronistic events:
(a) a coincidence between mental content (thought or feeling) and an outer event; (b) a dream or vision which coincides with an event that is taking place at a distance and verified later; and (c) an image (dream, vision, or premonition) about something that will happen in the future, which then does occur. Following are examples from reunited families:

> *I am an adoptee who found some of my maternal family 10 years ago. My birthmother was deceased by the time I found them. One of the first things I asked was, "When did she die?" I could not wait to go home to see if I had written a recognition of it in my journal. The dates were indeed the same. I remember that day very well, and I wrote in my journal, "I feel someone close to me has died."* (48fc)

> *In February 1990 I began having dreams that my mother was not well and that she was about to be diagnosed with a serious illness. In March 1990 I dreamed that she had been diagnosed with cancer and that she was not going to be living very long. I was trying very hard to find her. In October 1990 I said to the agency, "I feel like it's too late, that she has died, but I still need to find the family." When I finally did find my birth family in March 1991, I found that I was exactly right; my mother had been diagnosed with cancer in March 1990, and she died in September 1990.* (53fc)

Central to Jung's theory was the affirmation that what he called *archetypes* (dispositions of the *collective unconscious* with strong psychic energy) are the *organizers* in instincts, impulses, and spiritual elements for the unity of personality. They transcend space and time, leading to internal-external parallels in psychic and physical events. Jung understood the unconscious mind to have two dimensions: the *personal unconscious*, containing material related to ideas and impressions of one's personal life, temporarily lost to conscious memory, and thoughts too objectionable to be acknowledged in consciousness; and the *collective unconscious*, containing material beyond one's own experience, from a universal knowledge. Communication between the personal unconscious and the collective unconscious occurs by way of dreams, hunches, serendipitous encounters, or neurotic anxiety and fears. The collective unconscious works to compensate and balance. Communications from it are teleological, to propel one toward truth, honesty, and wholeness.

Jung thought that acausal events are related to these unconscious psychological processes. **Causality** is defined by objective knowledge from observation of a logical series of events that can generally be repeated. **Synchronicity** is different in that it is a subjective experience with significant timing and meaning to the participant. Each incident is unique and unrepeatable. Synchronicities act as clues to an underlying system that is ineffable, inexpressible, awesome, and numinous. "Numinous" is a term Jung borrowed from Rudolf Otto (1958), referring to that which humans experience when in contact with God or the holy. Jung believed the approach to the numinous to be true therapy that released one from the curse of pathology.

Like others before and after him, Jung (1960) kept a logbook of synchronicities. He wrote:

> *I have often come up against the phenomena in question, and could convince myself how much these inner experiences meant to my patients. In most cases they were things which people do not talk about for fear of exposing themselves to thoughtless ridicule. I was amazed to see how many people have had experiences of this kind, and how carefully the secret was guarded.* (p. 420)

If an adoptee and his birth family never reunite, they are unable to confirm the matching convergence of their lives at those critical points Koestler (1972) called "confluential events" (p. 140). But for those who do find each other, the revealed coincidences are more than chance; they take on numinosity and become synchronicities. Is it possible that what might seem to be a series of discrete events is in actuality a single, archetypal composite?

For the purposes of this book, the operational definition of *synchronicity* has two consistent components: (a) a *coincidence*, "a notable concurrence of events or circumstances without apparent causal connection"; and (b) inherent, subjective *meaning*, evidenced by feelings of surprise and *awe*, "solemn and reverential wonder" (Oxford Dictionary,

1989), **in the reunited family members when such a coincidence is discovered.**

To an outsider the meaning or significance may range from nonexistent to trivial to archetypal. For the participants, the *meaning* is "intent or spirit apart from the 'letter' of a statement" (Oxford). A synchronicity may arise from a choice, a chance, or a change; it may be a name, an encounter, an event, a characteristic, or a hunch that is identical, slightly similar, or simply surprising. For example: An unexpected gesture, a misspelled word, or the selection of a boyfriend seems to produce the same awesome feeling of an enduring connection as would a vivid premonition of crisis or the precisely timed initiation of search activity:

> *When I first met my son, during our conversation, whenever he was puzzled about something, he would lean forward on his elbow and pull at his eyebrow, kind of a nervousness. This was a habit that his birthfather had! When I mentioned it later, he said that his adoptive mother had always commented about it. It was irritating to her, and nobody else in the family did it. (65fp)*

> *My mother and I are both poor spellers, and we misspell the same simple words. I remember when I got the first letter from my mother and left it on the kitchen counter. My twins came home from school and said, "Who are you writing to, Mom?" Our handwriting is identical too! (18fc)*

> *My daughter's boyfriend's name was Frank; my first boyfriend's name was Frank. She recently broke up with him and is now dating a young man who operates a pool cleaning and maintenance company. Guess what my second boyfriend did? Right! (38fp)*

Coincidence as Synchronicity

COINCIDENCE AND KAMMERER'S LAW OF SERIALITY

Paul Kammerer was an Austrian biologist whose studies had an influence on Jung's ideas of synchronicity. While Jung thought that all synchronistic phenomena which had no apparent physical causality were related to unconscious psychological processes, Kammerer rejected mentalistic and extrasensory explanations in favor of simple physical analogies for correlation by affinity. Nevertheless, both scientists regarded the principle of acausality to be of equal rank with causality in the interaction of man and his world.

In what began as a hobby, Kammerer kept a logbook of coincidences for 20 years and developed a theory published in 1919, *Das Gesetz der Serie: Eine Lehre von den Wiederholungen im Lebens--und im Weltgeschehen* [The Law of Seriality: A Doctrine of Repetitions in Events in Life and Society]. It was the German equivalent of the universal comment on accidents, "When it rains, it pours." The 486-page book has no complete English translation to date, although Arthur Koestler summarized its principles in his biography of Kammerer, *The Case of the Midwife Toad* (1971), and in *The Roots of Coincidence* (1972). A few more passages were translated for my investigation.

Definition of the law of seriality: Kammerer defined the law of seriality as an **acausal, unifying principle** at work in the universe. Just as real and mysterious as universal gravity, which acts indiscriminately on all mass, this principle differs in **correlating by affinity**, pulling toward unity, and producing concurrent or serial events in space and time. The affinity or likeness may be in symbols, function, form, or substance. "We thus arrive at the image of a world-mosaic or cosmic kaleidoscope, which, in spite of constant shufflings and rearrangements, also *takes care of bringing like and like together*" [emphasis added] (Kammerer, 1919, p. 165).

Kammerer's log of coincidences focused almost exclusively on a theme, an idea, or a pattern of repetitive events: names, words, numbers, letters, clothing, a subject of conversation, dreams, or disasters. He became convinced that the sequences he had discovered and labeled, the law of seriality, gave evidence of a previously unknown objective principle of nature, as fundamental as those of physics, a kind of inertia by which similar events are repeated, operating independent of physical causation:

> The fulfillment of wishes and premonitions; answers to prayers, whether hoped for or unhoped for; deliverance from oppression and danger ("when need is greatest, God is nearest"); and the materialization of dreams and daydreams, which then appear to be prophetic, are related to this type of seriality. The knowledge of a heretofore unobserved natural regularity in this case promises an explanation, whereas earlier only a belief in miracles found acceptance. (Kammerer, 1919, pp. 39-40)

He regarded seriality as "ubiquitous and continuous in life, nature, and cosmos. It is the umbilical cord that connects thought, feeling, science, and art with the womb of the universe which gave birth to them" (Kammerer, 1919, p. 456). That statement has graphic application to this study, in which the mother-child umbilical cord plays a role in what is felt by many to be a continuing conscious or unconscious connection.

In the first half of *Das Gesetz der Serie*, Kammerer presented a careful taxonomy of 100 instances of coincidental seriality. Non-causal concurrences of names, numbers, words, situations, and so forth were given a typology. In an objective, scientific manner, he provided a morphology, classifying by order (number of sequential coincidences), power (number of parallel or concurrent coincidences), and their number of similar attributes or parameters. His categories were designed to encompass even those instances where several coincidences flow into and enfold each other, where a beginning and an end to enumeration seem impossible. He classified the structural relationships of seriality as homologous or analogous; pure or hybrid; cyclic, phasic, or alternating, and so forth. An example of what he called a concurrence of the third power is the following account of three nearly simultaneous events between an adoption-separated mother and daughter:

> In May 1985 I became involved with Amnesty International in California; at the same time, my mother started the chapter of Amnesty International in her area of Canada. Also in May 1985 I first contacted the adoption agency; my mother had contacted the agency the same week, but they didn't tell us. I was thinking, "You're exactly double my age," because I was 21 at the time. "I'm the same age you were when you had me." My sister later told me, "That's exactly what she said." I found the family after my mother's death. (53fc)

The experiences of this particular family demonstrate the difficulty of counting enfolding coincidences, where one leads directly into the next. This is a daughter who had recurring, simultaneously timed dreams of her mother's illness, diagnosis, and death. The adoption agency refused to help her find her mother, saying she was making an emotional connection that wasn't there. Finally:

> I reached the family on my sister's birthday. She had just said to her girlfriend that she lived with at the university, "My birthday wish is that my sister will find me." I happened to be ringing her old house at that very minute. She was ecstatic. (53fc)

Kammerer's concept of the pulling of like and like toward unity may be demonstrated by coincidences of location in migration, residence, vacation, and search activity. Two examples convey the ways in which parents and children were drawn together:

> My daughter, who was adopted in Nebraska, recently found her birthmother after a three-year search. The mother contacted me, and our first surprising discoveries are: My daughter works in the film business, as I do; she lives in Los Angeles, as I do, and lives about five blocks from me. When she first visited me, it turned out she had looked at the apartments I live in when she was first looking for a place to live, but they were too expensive; she found another place, which happened to be an apartment that I looked at previously. We use the same bank and stores, due to our proximity. Go figure! (69mp)

> I had been searching for my mother for a year and getting nowhere. One day at work a co-worker asked if I was having any luck. Another woman who worked there overheard us and said, "Luck about what?" I took out my birth certificate, and the woman said, "I might know somebody who can help." She asked me for a baby picture and took it home to compare with one she had. She was shocked. She was my mother! She had been trying to find me for nearly 20 years. It is a large city [metroplex area of 230,000 population], and I had started working at this store just a few days before she did. We had worked there on different shifts for six months before our wonderful discovery. And that's not all: Another girl that we worked with was raised by my birthfather! She knew exactly where he was. So it was amazing; all in one day I found my mother and knew where my father was too. (64fc)

Perhaps meaningful synchronicities do not easily lend themselves to categorization but are holistic, as Jung maintained. Yet Koestler (1972), in his admiration for the unorthodox brilliance of Kammerer, reminded the skeptic that although some chapters of the book may contain naive errors in physics,

> *This first attempt at a systematic classification of coincidental events may find some unexpected applications at some future date. These things happen in science. It may also be the reason why Einstein gave a favourable opinion of the book . . . He may have remembered that the non-Euclidian geometries, invented by earlier mathematicians more or less as a game, provided the basis for his relativistic cosmology.* (pp. 87-88)

Einstein called Kammerer's work "original and by no means absurd" (Przibram, 1926, cited in Koestler, 1972, p. 87). It has been said that Jung's concept of synchronicity came to him during a dinner conversation with Einstein in the 1920s (Combs & Holland, 1990). One might speculate if their discussion touched on the ideas of their contemporaries, Kammerer and Freud. Freud, who later disagreed sharply with Jung, wrote in an essay titled *The "Uncanny"* (1919/1963) about the recurrence of names, situations, things, and events. His preliminary conclusion was that the uncanny experience proceeds from something familiar which has been repressed. He made a brief comment about Kammerer: "Not long ago an ingenious scientist attempted to reduce coincidences of this kind to certain laws, and so deprive them of their uncanny effect. I will not venture to decide whether he has succeeded or not" (pp. 43-44).

KAMMERER AND ADOPTION

Kammerer was a Lamarckian whose beliefs put him in ill-fated opposition to the leading mechanistic biologists of his day. His preoccupations apply to the current topic in another way: He included a chapter on "Inheritance and Child Adoption" in *The Inheritance of Acquired Characteristics* (1924). He crudely stated:

> *Verily, one could say that child adoption is one of the most favorite, and at the same time most constructive, indoor sports of the American nation. In more than one respect, this is an interesting product of the great international melting pot. . . . Couldn't this child bring into the well-guarded family of his benefactor harmful dispositions and perhaps hereditary instinctive criminality, which even in an environment of a most law-abiding family would assert themselves irresistibly?* (p. 295)

He went on to say, however, that social deprivation and unhealthy surroundings were to blame for "crowding healthily inclined individuals into a life of crime . . . vices, and diseases" (p. 297), and that he hoped a degenerative inheritance could slowly be corrected by an improved environment, loving care, and thorough education. Kammerer (1924) believed that *inheritance* was the complex of environmental impressions imprinted on past generations; *environment* he referred to as the relatively minimal number of impressions engraved on an individual during his lifetime (p. 299). Earnshaw's (1987) postulation of family time-tagged DNA that reflects both inherited and shared emotional crises echoes some of Kammerer's thinking (see Chapter 13).

8
Connected by a Cosmic Designer?

> ❖ *The most beautiful thing we can experience is the mysterious. It is the source of all true art and science. He to whom this emotion is a stranger, who can no longer pause to wonder and stand rapt in awe, is as good as dead: his eyes are closed. This insight into the mystery of life, coupled though it be with fear, has also given rise to religion. To know what is impenetrable to us really exists, manifesting itself as the highest wisdom and the most radiant beauty which our dull faculties can comprehend only in their most primitive forms--this knowledge, this feeling is at the center of true religiousness.* (Albert Einstein, *What I Believe*, 1930)

When a mother has a premonition that her child is in danger, or an adoptee moves across the country for no logical reason, is there a higher force directing them? After the peak experience of reunion, families often seek philosophical answers to the mysteries of nature and the transcendent essence of the human spirit:

> *I feel that God led me in the right way, because there were so many things that could have prevented me from ever finding my son.* (65fp)

> *I don't have many relatives, so it was like God planned our reunion that way, so I wouldn't be alone. I believe that everything was planned.* (67fc)

Humans have long contemplated with awe their place in the timeless reality of the cosmos (cosmology), the enigma of consciousness, the origin and limits of knowledge (epistemology), and the ultimate nature of being (ontology). In our era of modern science and space exploration, vast amounts of data are still being gathered for clues to the absolute laws of the universe, final causes and ultimate design (teleology), and the character of the One that formulated them (theology). Reunited families are wondering too.

COSMOLOGY

❖ *Like the meridians as they approach the poles, science, philosophy, and religion are bound to converge as they draw nearer to the whole.*
(Teilhard de Chardin, *A Phenomenon of Man*, 1959)

About 530 BC, Pythagoras set up his secret Greek school in Croton in southern Italy, teaching that number or quantity was the key to unlocking all human and cosmic order. Just as music depends on the length and tuning of strings on an instrument, the Pythagoreans believed that universal mathematical relationships could also incorporate laws of beauty, goodness, and truth. There is a current resurgence of interest in the mysticism of Hebrew kabbalistic literature of the late Middle Ages. *Sefer Yezirah* [The Book of Creation] suggested that letters and numbers are like elements, and that they have ontological value; they act as operational agents that create reality and produce being (Friedman, 1977). A mother described the meaning she found in numbers:

> *My son and I were both living at 507--different streets in different cities-- but we both lived at the same house number. The last four digits of his telephone number (6518) were the year in which he was born and my age at the time he was born.* (49fp)

Kammerer's (1919) investigation of natural cyclic behavior included the significance of the number seven: in Pythagorean symbolism evidenced by the repetition of seven notes in the musical scale; and in biblical symbolism evidenced by completeness, perfection, and the seven-day week. Freud believed in 23- and 27-day cycles that combined to affect behavior. The scope of this book does not permit delving into the voluminous medical and biological material on lunar, solar, circadian, and geomagnetic rhythms known to affect man, and a thorough exploration of their influence on homing or reunion.

Roger Penrose, the Rouse Ball Professor of Mathematics at the University of Oxford, worked on the puzzles of cosmology with his friend, Stephen Hawking, the Lucasian Professor of Mathematics at Cambridge University. They demonstrated that not only space-time, but matter and energy had a singular beginning; if cause and effect existed before time, a pre-existent creative mind is implied (Hawking & Penrose, 1970).

Penrose (1989) is known for his rigorous formulation and proof of a precise mathematical theorem showing that space-time singularities are inevitable in every black hole, where the laws of physics no longer apply. Like a number of intuitive experiences in the family stories, the key criterion in his solution came to his mind during a lull in conversation on a different subject, while walking across a road with a colleague. The idea subsided into his unconscious as conversation resumed, but later in the day he had an unaccountable feeling of elation, and finally pulled to consciousness the idea he subsequently called a "trapped surface" (p. 421). Another of his intuitive discoveries is that of the three-dimensional Penrose tiles, quasi crystals underlying a strange new kind of matter. Such serendipitous discoveries are as common in the annals of science history (Roberts, 1989) as they are in search and reunion stories. Where do they originate?

Algorithms. Penrose believes there is a level beyond quantum mechanics in which are embedded the universal truths of algorithms. When mathematicians make discoveries, they are merely uncovering truths which are already there, as in Plato's (360 BC) ideal world of mathematical concepts, accessible only by the intellect. "There must be some deep underlying reason for the accord between mathematics and physics, i.e. between Plato's world and the physical world," said Penrose (1989, p. 430). Further, he declared that for algorithms to exist, they require an interpretation, or a decoding of the arrangements, "and that will depend upon the 'language' in which the algorithms are written. Again *a pre-existing mind seems to be required* [emphasis added], in order to 'understand' the language, and we are back where we were" (pp. 429-430).

In a discussion of the mind-body problem and conscious-unconscious activities of the brain, Penrose (1989) stated that while distinctions are not always clear, "My own line of reasoning has been that unconscious processes could well be algorithmic, but at a very complicated level that is monstrously difficult to disentangle in detail" (p. 411), and "the hallmark of consciousness is a non-algorithmic forming of judgements" (p. 413). He would seem to be stating Jung's idea of archetypes and the collective unconscious in different language and an expanded framework.

HOLOMOVEMENT

Jung used a metaphor of consciousness rising like an island from the sea of the unconscious. Physicist David Bohm (1980) chose an analogy of a rippling vortex in water for his theory of holomovement. It involves new assumptions about the nature of matter and postulates the universe as a living organism, an unfolding and enfolding, non-mechanistic network of interconnections that are independent of time or space proximity. Bohm theorized that the world perceived by the senses and by scientific instruments, the *unfolded or explicate order*, is just a fraction of reality. It emerges from or is contained in a larger and generative source, the *enfolded or implicate order*. Like a hologram in which light waves in movement are directly recorded, information about an entire object moves and is dynamically enfolded in all of space, and is then unfolded in an image.

What does this infer about the anomalous perception of information and the movement of separated family members toward each other? In their own search for wholeness, self, or the lost object, the movement toward each other, like the arrows on a Möbius band, seems primary to their individuation. The secondary entities that unfold and become enfolded again, appearing and disappearing at various times, include dreams, hunches, mental states, ideas, fantasies, words, names, and objects. In the culmination of the search process, a mother and child may

find that the essential ingredient to their individuation was not only in realizing the whole again, but in seeing themselves as authentic, valuable parts.

Following is one male adoptee's story of his sense of completion:

> *At age 37, as soon as I heard it was true I was adopted, I instantly had a void feeling deep within me. I immediately felt an emptiness and that a part of me was missing. My primary desire and need of finding and meeting my birthmother has become a reality, and now I feel a complete person. The future offers me the opportunity to continue to know my birthmother, while my relationship with my mom who raised me is fine. I am also going to help others learn where to research, and hopefully I will be able to help others find their biological families. I simply feel wonderful!* (63mc)

Louis Zinkin (1987), a London Jungian analyst, developed the holographic model for analytical psychology, concluding that physics has now meshed with Jung's idea of synchronicity, and that everything is interconnected through an acausal principle. Zinkin commented that the sense of a mother and infant being simultaneously one and two is usual and normal, and not an illusion. In spite of cultural differences in sleeping together or in separate rooms,

> *In all cultures, the sensitive mother recognises that she and her baby are true 'partners' who are never really 'apart.' Both recognise that though each is part of the other, each is also whole while being a part of the greater whole. . . . both participate in the holographic-like pattern which involves them both.* (p. 19)

It has been shown with quantum particles that the behavior of one may be predicted from the behavior of another, even at remote distances, with no possibility of actual causation. Do genetically related organisms affect each other at a distance? Two further incidents seem to suggest that they do:

> *My daughter and I were both in bike accidents in 1971. She fell off her bike and broke her front tooth, and I went flying over my bike and broke my front tooth. When she told me she had a cap on her front tooth, I said, "So do I!"* (32fp)

> As a small child in the third grade, in the year 1943, I became obsessed with someday having my own farm. I went to the library almost on a daily basis to read everything I could on the subject of raising animals and farming. After finding my paternal family, I found that they and all their forebears had been farmers. It was in 1943 that they finally sold their farm to move into the city, as they were elderly. Both paternal grandparents died shortly afterward. (I had never been exposed to farming, as my adoptive family were always city folk.) (42fc)

If there were a cause for the quantum influence or the synchronous event, it would have to be some form of as-yet-unknown communication that is faster than the speed of light (Bohm, 1980; Bohm & Peat, 1987).

TIME

Michael Shallis (1983), who first was a film director, then became interested in physics and received a doctorate in astrophysics, is a tutor in the Department for External Studies at the University of Oxford. He wrote of anomalistic psychology, metaphysics, the phenomenon of meaningful coincidence, and newly researched concepts of time:

> Coincidence as a temporal phenomenon is a wonderful example of time's duality. If the concept of the dual nature of light as both wave and particle is acceptable, then coincidences should help in the acceptance of the no more strange idea that time displays the duality of the connected, linear, causal side of its nature and its acausal, unconnected aspect. (p. 140)

Shallis (1983) posed questions which may be relevant to the parent-child nexus and the coincidence of dates in this study: Is time imbedded in a timeless matrix that we can occasionally perceive? Does time run backward as well as forward, but normally only one way of the flow can be detected? Are the phenomena of timelessness, eternity, time reversal, precognition, mixed-up times, and even systems operating outside time real? How is it that, although man may spatialize it for scientific convenience, there is one property of time that remains different from space: its unidirectionality? Can information travel faster than the speed of light? Not so far as is known, but, if so, it could defy time and go forward or backward. Shallis (1983) views time as symbolic of a deeper reality, and a synchronicity "may just be nature pointing out time's own meaning" (p. 152). Following is an illustrative case of meaningful information extended over time and condensed in space, on a single piece of paper:

> I named my daughter Justine at birth. My mother used to take orders and knit Christmas stockings, and she would chart the names on graph paper. Two years after the surrender, she had to chart a stocking for someone named Justine. Now, going years on: Mother saved all the names she charted on a large piece of graph paper. A year or two after our reunion, when she was going through some papers, she found right under the name Justine the name Kimberly that she had charted for someone else. That was the name given to my daughter by the adoptive family! Right under that name she had charted the names John and Terry; those were the adoptive parents' names. On that single piece of paper, over a period of eight years, appeared those four names together! She handed it to me, and it was **very eerie**. (54fp)

Gardner Murphy (1989), the eclectic social psychologist who directed research at the Menninger Foundation, wrote extensively in his exploration of the scientific challenge to create a field theory for what appeared to be telepathic and clairvoyant occurrences outside a living organic system, concluding that inadequate definitions of time and space were at the heart of the problem, and "we confront a 'rubber sheet' type of phenomenon in which the events with which we make contact are not really 'at a distance,' or 'in the future'" (p. 19).

THE FAMILY AS A LIVING SYSTEM

General living systems theory (Miller, 1978) is a recent interdisciplinary effort to establish a communication network for independent work in the search for universals, from the submicroscopic to the cellular, from the organism to its relationships, from the family to the supranational system, and beyond to the harmony of the cosmos. Murphy (1989) insisted that the social sciences should not be compartmentalized and that the study of any whole organism could best be understood through a study of its origins:

> If replication on every level and repetitive structural patterns are demonstrated among the multiple levels of organization, what would this imply? That some ancient but successful model has been stamped out of a master template? That it has been duplicated through time and space; that its basic structures have produced basic functions; that it somehow

accounts for the swing of the Pleiades, the splitting of the DNA helix, the birth and death of a man? If a basic relationship between the animate and the inanimate, between the small and the large does exist, such order could hardly be called accidental or incidental. . . . **What is the nature of the ultimate power which created the world without and the world within?** [emphasis added]. (pp. 270-271)

There is both thought and felt to be some sort of incessant, dynamic interaction between the universe and mankind, but at the present time science is just as baffled at its intent or extent as are the reunited families. The common tides of birth and death, sleeping and waking, remain as tantalizingly mysterious as the parent-child nexus:

My mother gave birth to another baby girl on my birthday, two years later. (33fc)

My father died on my son's 24th birthday, which is what made me aggressively hunt for him, rather than just wait for him to respond to having my name listed in reunion registries. When something like that happens, you feel the person who died is happy in your meeting another part of your own family whom you've never met before. You have a loss, but you are also finding someone at the same time. When I first met my son, I felt like a weight was lifted off my shoulders. (49fp)

John Gribbin (1984), who has a doctorate in astrophysics, wrote of recent research in quantum theory leading to the idea of a universal system, with particles interacting from the time of creation's initial big bang. His general statement has philosophical application to the specific unity of mother and child: "Particles that were once together in an interaction remain in some sense parts of a single system, which responds together in future interactions" (p. 229). Freud went one step further and said that "an instinct is an urge inherent in organic life to restore an earlier state of things" (1920/1955, p. 35), and modern psychiatry has spoken of a regression to the union of an infant with its mother as the ultimate essence of the mystical state.

TELEOLOGY

❖ *We dance 'round in a ring and suppose
But the Secret sits in the middle and knows.*
(Robert Frost, *The Secret Sits*, 1945)

Teleology, an aspect of metaphysics, is the doctrine or study of ends or final causes, especially as related to the evidences of design or purpose in nature. As part of the philosophy of vitalism (as opposed to mechanism), natural phenomena are thought to be determined not only by mechanical causes but by an overall purpose, directed toward a definite end. Synchronicity was described by Combs and Holland (1990) as a riddle to be lightheartedly enjoyed as the playful purpose of a trickster, rather than the rational Logos of classical Greece and Rome, but they concluded:

> *The inescapable insinuation of synchronicity, however, is that the cosmos is undergirded by teleology. Synchronicity reminds us of this order and beckons us to enter into it. Purpose in the form of synchronistic coincidences finds us even in the banalities of our daily routines. . . . Its purpose cannot in the end be grasped with the rational mind. It must be lived with one's whole being.* (p. 144)

In the union/loss/reunion experience, when time and teleology touch, as in a flash across a Möbius band, does a mechanical DNA code function according to a metadimensional, master design? Will a glimpse into the contacts between members of a separated family system increase our knowledge not only of immediate reality but also of infinite teleology and order?

THEOLOGY AND THE COLLECTIVE UNCONSCIOUS: NAMES AND CONCEPTS

❖ *We are most likely to find the correct names in the nature of the eternal and absolute; for there the names ought to have been given with the greatest care, and perhaps some of them were given by a power more divine than is that of men.* (Plato, *Cratylus*)

Twentieth-century Christian philosopher, Francis A. Schaeffer (1968), explained Jung's collective unconscious as a collective cultural consciousness or memory related to words. He felt it was composed of two parts: "a collective memory of a specific race, and a collective memory of all men as to what man is and what reality is" (p. 182). Because man thinks and communicates in language, as a symbol system it keeps alive a deep, unconscious world view of humanity's uniqueness and the existence of God. As one example, Schaeffer pointed to the common use even by atheists of curses in the name of God, and not a lesser being, as "a deeper yet simpler explanation than Jung's view of god as the supreme archetype arising (according to him) out of the evolution of the race. . . . Thus man, in his *language*, 'remembers' (regardless of his personal belief) that God does exist" (p. 182).

Psychiatrist M. Scott Peck (1978) went further: "In my vision the collective unconscious is God; the conscious is man as individual; and the personal unconscious is the interface between them" (p. 282). This may infer that anomalous information entering the personal unconscious of separated family members is like prayer or communication between man and God.

The storytellers in this collection are from nations with a Judeo-Christian heritage, in whose biblical writings the meaning of a name gave clues to a person's character. For example, God, through the angel Gabriel, gave instructions to Mary (Miriam) and Joseph to name his son Jesus (Yeshua), the Hebrew word meaning "salvation," for the reason that "he will save his people from their sins" (Matthew 1:21b, NIV).

In Judaism, the Tetragrammaton, the ineffable name of YHVH, is not to be spoken or read aloud and thus taken in vain. In the time of Temple worship in Jerusalem, it was uttered only by the high priest on the Day of Atonement. Today, worshippers use a substitute such as Adonai (Lord), or simply Hashem (The Name). The exact significance of the word YHVH cannot be decided, although the concept of "being" is in its root. It has been variably interpreted as: the existing, absolute, and unchangeable one; the giver of existence, who causes, the creator; the one ever coming into manifestation; and the inexplicable "I am who I am" (Brown, Driver, & Briggs, 1979, p. 218).

In certain other religions, in order to call upon a spirit or gain its approval for a priest's request, it is necessary to call it by name. A name's active or magical power is also found in traditional fairy tales, when to discover someone's name meant to gain power over him. In ancient Egypt, to scratch the name from a tomb was equated with removing the person from eternal life. This may be related to the scriptural concept of sinners' names being blotted from the Book of Life (Exodus 32:33; Revelation 3:5).

In Eastern meditation, the repetition of a mantra, a carefully chosen word or name, is thought to play a role in transforming consciousness and individual reality. The belief holds that the specific vibrations which resonate in the thoughts of the mind, as well as physically in the chest and nasal cavities, have power and must be chosen in harmony with mind, body, and the universe. The power of verbal symbols for objects or persons is that they focus attention on otherwise nebulous concepts, explained F. David Peat (1987): **"Names could be thought of as the first categories, but they are not simply passive, descriptive sounds or referential symbols, for, according to these myths, they have an active quality that is able to produce order out of chaos"** (pp. 208-209).

Creation accounts of various cultures equate the appearance of order with the power of the words used in naming the distinctions. "And God said, 'Let there be light,' and there was light" (Genesis 1:3, NIV). The single Hebrew word OLAM enfolds and unfolds meanings of space, time, and creation: It means the universe, infinity past and future, and continuous existence. The same root is used for a young man and a young woman who are sexually mature, or capable of the creation of offspring (Brown, Driver, & Briggs, 1979, pp. 761-763).

Who can begin to fathom the rich symbolization and dynamic movement contained in one such word . . . or in an individual's name?

9
Connection by Names

Rudolf

> My son had a nickname that his adoptive brother called him when he was younger--Rudolf. At our recent reunion I told him what my father's name was: Rudolf Matthew, but he chose to be called Matt. He had been named Rudolf after his own father. So my son's nickname was the same as both his grandfather and his great-grandfather! (49fp)

Human beings attach great significance to words and names. They are the only species known capable of giving individual names to everything from their children to pets, streets, athletic teams, and hurricanes. Until the late Middle Ages, when hereditary last names came into English usage, only one name was given to a person. A common custom in many cultures is to name a child for relatives. It is surprising and meaningful, then, when family names appear without human foreknowledge in a person who has lived apart from his birth ancestors:

> My son's adoptive parents happened to choose as his middle name the name of my grandfather, who died six weeks after he was born. (10fp)

> My husband, a birthfather, found his son's adoptive name is the same as his. (26fo)

Many birthmothers were never told they were permitted to name their babies before being separated by adoption, and frequently the original birth certificate was inscribed simply "Baby Girl Jones." The last name might have been the family name of the birthmother, the birthfather, or often a pseudonym given the mother by a maternity home worker. Whether or not she officially named her baby, each mother knows the name by which she will remember this precious life and carries it with her, bringing it to her conscious mind on the birthday anniversary or other occasions:

> *When I was carrying my baby I always called her "my little angel spirit" or "my little angel." The name given to her by her new parents is Angela. I thought of the connection right away, but always kept the story to myself.* (60fp)

Because most adoptees have no access to their original birth certificates, they do not know the names given to them by their mothers. When engaged in a search, therefore, it is a breath-taking moment when the real name of the other person is learned: Instead of a pseudonym, the adoptee now knows the mother's name; instead of a fantasy, the birth family has a named child for whom to search. The experience of name-learning is often emotion-laden, and just as marked in the mind as, for example, the day President John F. Kennedy was killed. Ordinarily each family member can vividly recall where he or she was, with the accompanying kinesthetic reactions, when first reading or hearing a significant lost name:

> *The day I found out my birth name, I experienced an emotional breakdown. That day was my birthmother's 48th birthday.* (34fc)

After reunion, names are prominent in the meaning-making of the renewed connection, in effect producing order out of chaos. They are usually the first, most obvious evidence of uncanny similarities:

> *I found an older sister with the same name as one of my daughters: Kimberly. My daughter's second name is Rochelle; my mother and all of her family came from the town of Rochelle. I have an adoptive brother named Daryl; my sister, Kimberly, married a husband named Daryl. I also have both an adoptive and a birth sister called Suzie.* (56mc)

During the time of my search, every time I would seek information through the adoption agency, I would be taken aback at the reaction. It was only later, at reunion, that I learned the adoptive mother shares my same name, Audrey. She also kept the same name for our daughter that I had given her--Jean Ann. (6fp)

Thirty-two of the original 70 families who contributed to my study had encountered similar names, including many unusual ones. There were 22 meaningful matches between adoptive and birth families, and 10 between birth relatives. Seventeen had more than one or runs of multiple matches. Four sets of birth siblings chose the same names for their actual (or desired) children. Four mothers named another child by the unknown, adoptive name of the first-born. Four adoptees in some way knew or made unusual use of their mothers' names, as for imaginary friends.

Following, in the storytellers' own words, are further examples of the coincidental network of names they uncovered:

My name is <u>Chris</u>tine. Last year I contacted the agency that handled my son's adoption to request non-identifying information about him and his adoptive family. I found out that my son was named <u>Chris</u>topher. (I had named him Ben.) (12fp)

My middle name is Lee. My daughter's adoptive father's middle name is Lee, and she gave her son the middle name of Lee. (14fp)

My name on my papers (before adoption) is Deborah Marie. I now know that my oldest half sister had a child at 15. She put the baby up for adoption, but not before naming her Deborah Marie. She knew nothing about me. Also, my birthmother says she didn't name me and doesn't know how I came to be Deborah Marie! My full sister also put a child up for adoption. The family that adopted her named her Theresa; that's our natural mother's name. (51fc)

I had an imaginary friend named Susan. One sister I have found is named Susan! I once lived on Graham Road. I later learned my name had been Graham. Several of my pets had family names. (48fc)

SYNCHRONICITY AND REUNION

My mother and I have dogs with exactly the same name: Tasha. (5fc)

Seven months before I found my mother, I bought a horse that already had the name of Rose. My mother's name is Rose. (58fc)

A grim situation may burst with elements of therapeutic laughter. Combs and Holland (1990) described synchronicity like the work of Hermes the Trickster. A good laugh after the rigors of separation, search, and reunion is prompted by many of the tangles of coincidence, as shown in this chain of names:

> The name for me on my adoption decree is John. My adoptive mother later named me John after her grandfather. My adoptive father's name was Jack. My birthmother later married a man named John. Their son's name is Sean. We look alike. Their older daughter's husband was named John. When I got to know their younger daughter, I learned her boyfriend's name was John. When I was in college I went out on a couple of platonic dates with a woman named Mary. I ran into her again about seven years later. At that time she [mistakenly] told someone that she and I had been lovers. When I met Sean for the first time, about seven years after that, he told me that **he** and Mary had been lovers in college! (20mc)

If the siblings in the following stories had been raised together, social custom would have discouraged their choosing the same names for their children. The fact that they never knew each other provided freedom for a possible genetic influence to work:

My half sister's children are named Kristy and Katy, and mine are Kris and Kathryn! (7fc)

When I was pregnant with my second child, my first choice for a boy's name was Paul Matthew. (I wrote it down and still have that scrap of paper.) I had a girl. I have now found out that my sister gave birth to a boy shortly before that, and his name is Paul Matthew! (31fs)

My husband and I have no children. If I were to have had a daughter, I would have named her Maxine. My identical twin sister, with whom I have been reunited, had named her daughter Maxine. (67fc)

When my wife and I were to have our second child in June, we chose the name James Barton for a boy; we had a girl. When I found my birthmother in October, I found out her married last name is Barton. My five-year-old daughter is named Lisa Natalie; my half brother has a daughter named Natalie. My birthfather's wife's name is Lillian; my first wife's name is Lillian. The older sister I grew up with in my adoptive family (she was not adopted) was born on my birthfather's birthday; she is named Roberta but goes by the name Bobbie. My birthmother also has an older sister named Roberta who goes by the name Bobbie. (63mc)

The preceding account demonstrates not only the two brothers' naming a daughter Natalie, but a continuous unfolding of one coincidence into another between the birth and adoptive families. Additional anecdotes show meaningful seriality in similar names in adoptive and birth families:

My adoptive father and his father are both named George; my natural grandfather's name is George as well. My natural mother's name is Beverly, and my natural father's name is Bruce; my adoptive sister's name is Beverly, and she married a man named Bruce. When we put this together, we thought it was weird. (23fc)

Jessie was my birthmother's mother's name; Jessie was also my adoptive father's mother's name. (19fc)

My son was named Kent, and his adoptive sister was named Melissa. His birthfather's sister also named two of her children Kent and Melissa (his cousins). (65fp)

When a natural sister was born into my daughter's adoptive family, she was given the honor of naming the baby. The name she picked is the same as that of her birth cousin and a great-aunt. (68fp)

My half sister named a daughter the same as my name. When my youngest daughter was born, my husband I were trying to think of a name for her and were thinking of long names such as Meredith. My adoptive mother makes each child a special Christmas stocking with his or her name on top of it, so she offhandedly said, "Why don't you name her something simple like Bobbie Sue or Mary Jo?" I came to find out that my birth name was Mary Jo! (29fc)

As I live in New Zealand, and my recently contacted son lives in South Australia, we haven't yet been able to meet, but that will come. Meanwhile we have received each other's first letter and had a two-hour telephone conversation. I think you could call it an amazing coincidence that his name is Alan Paul (but he's called Paul). Both his natural father and adoptive father are called Alan! My name is Margaret, and his adoptive mother's middle name is Margaret. My son named his second daughter, born this year on my birthday, Kelly Margaret. [The first name is quite similar to this birthmother's married name.] (27fp)

The following four cases represent birthmothers who named a subsequent child by the unknown, adoptive name of the first:

When I first decided I was going to search, I called the home for unwed mothers, and the same nun that was running the place was still there. I started a conversation with her. She asked if I had any other children, and I said that I had two sons, and that when I was 43 I had another daughter, and I named her Jamie Ann Marie. She said, "Oh, I don't believe it! I don't believe it!" I asked, "What?" And she said, "They named your daughter Ann Marie." I don't know what possessed me to name my later daughter Jamie Ann Marie, giving her three names. The night she was born, it was a difficult delivery. She was three weeks early, had deep breathing difficulties, and for some reason I thought she wasn't going to live. I called my twin sister, and she said that she had to give her daughter two middle names, in order to include a saint's name. I was going to name my daughter Jamie Ann, so I said, "Well, I'll name her Jamie Ann Marie, and I'll get everything in there."

Then when I found out--the same name--I just **knew** I was going to find her! [Later, in locating the adoptive family's address,] I nearly fell on the floor, because the name of the street was Simon Drive; Simon was the first name of her birthfather! And that wasn't enough: the adoptive father's name is Tom--the name of the fellow that left me on the rebound from Simon. And then, as if that isn't enough: her adoptive mother's name is Joan--my twin sister's name. (32fp)

My mother didn't know I was named Ann by my adoptive parents; she had named me Elizabeth. She also named her next daughter Elizabeth, and then she had Charlotte Ann. Now, as an adult having found my birth family, I have taken back the name Elizabeth, with Ann as my second name. I now share a name with each of my sisters. Another weird thing that really gave me goose bumps is this: My mother wrote in her first letter to me that her mother is called Gaggy; when little Elizabeth couldn't say Grandma, she said Gaggy. Well, in my adoptive family, I couldn't say Grandma, and I named mine Gagga. Never in my life have I met someone who has a grandmother called Gaggy or Gagga. So my adoptive grandmother is Gagga and my birth grandmother is Gaggy! (70fc)

After locating my daughter this year, it was noted that her adoptive name was Suzanne Marie. The daughter that I bore six years after her was named Suzanne Marie also; only when we said the name aloud, it didn't ring well with our last name, so my husband selected the middle name of Kay. However, had we not changed it, the name would have been exactly the same as the daughter I located after many years of search! I had given the name Victoria to my first-born, and she has decided to change her name, since she likes the name and since it was her "first" name. I am delighted that she is changing it, and it doesn't create peculiar situations when I discuss "Suzanne." Her adoptive parents are deceased. (13fp)

When I was in preschool I said, "I have a sister, but I don't 'member her name now." It was of sufficient seriousness to warrant a conference and written report to my adoptive parents, and I have a copy of it. I now know that a sister had been born into my birth family, and her name is the same as mine! (36fc)

[Her mother goes on to relate]: Not knowing, of course, the name given to our first daughter by her adoptive parents, two years later the name we gave our son included the sounds of her unusual name. A year after that, we named our younger daughter--and it is a shortened form of her sister's name and the name she has always preferred! I wonder if I received that name from the three-year-old's mind, and if our antennae were tuned for some kind of communication.

The older girl at one time shared an apartment with a best friend whose name was her unknown sister's middle name. We opened a new checking account at the same time our lost daughter got married, and her new last name was the same as the bank's. Her adoptive grandparents lived on a street that was my maiden name, and our daughter often wrote letters to that address. Her birthfather and adoptive brother both have the same uncommon middle name. On my daily walk in our neighborhood, my gaze would be drawn to a house with the sign "Fantaisie" and the last name of the owner. I would picture in my mind their granddaughter, who had attended the same school as our children. That girl's first and last name turned out to be exactly the name of our missing daughter!

At one point in my search, I made up a fictitious name to use in making an inquiry; it came to me "off the top of my head." I later learned the first two initials I had chosen were those of the adoptive father, and the last name had in exact order all the consonants of the adoptive mother's complete maiden name, except for a final suffix. Another time, during a telephone call to a clerk in Vital Statistics, when she had my daughter's name in front of her, I suddenly blurted out, "Is her first name _____?" She replied, "If it were, I could not tell you." What a surprise later to find out I was right, and it was an unpremeditated thought! (36fp)

Both the preceding and the following accounts are examples of a clairvoyant type of intuition, in which each mother knew and spoke her child's name in a spontaneous instant.

Connection by Names

I sent for and received hospital records from the hospital where I had given birth to my son 25 years before. I was surprised but pleased to receive 18 pages of documents, doctors' notes, and nurses' comments on both me and my baby. Also enclosed were his "certificate of live birth" and a copy of his footprints. The footprints were what really got to me emotionally, although because the labor had been very long and difficult, I was also very relieved to read that he had been a healthy baby with no problems from the birth experience. **I wrote a poem about him that day and superimposed copies of his little footprints on the poem. I thumbtacked it to the wall just inside my bedroom door.**
    A few months later (still before I had petitioned the courts), I walked into my bedroom to get ready for bed, causing the bottom edge of the poem to flutter in the breeze as I walked past. The movement caught my eye, and I glanced at the piece of paper on the wall, looking at the tiny footprints once again. At that moment, the name "Bryan" appeared in my thoughts out of nowhere. I felt somewhat shaken and confused as I continued to get ready for bed. Bryan is not the name I chose for this or either of my younger sons, so I decided it had to be the name given to him by his adoptive parents. I immediately told my 19-year-old (adopted) daughter about this revelation, saying that if it should possibly be true I wanted her as my witness that I did know his name. As I am sure you have guessed by now, Bryan is his name. (45fp)

The following section includes coincidences that, if not extrasensory, could have a prenatal memory cause, either from a mother's thoughts, or from the voices of persons speaking to her:

When my adoptive brother had his first child, he said, "What shall we name her?" I said, "Name her Nicole; it's such a beautiful name. Nicole, Nicole, I love the name Nicole!" So they used Nicole as her middle name. Now I know that my deceased birthmother's name is Nicole. (53fc)

When I was a little girl, and all through my teenage years, I always wanted to be named Maggie. Not for any particular reason, I just always wanted that name. When I located my original name in the state's birth register, I found that it was Margaret! So I really was a Maggie all along. (24fc)

I named my daughter, Rachel Virginia, for: (1) my adoptive mother, who died when I was seven--Virginia; and also for (2) my adoptive dad's mother--Rachel. After finding my birth family, I learned (3) my birthmother

> is Virginia; and (4) my birthfather had a grandmother Rachel. So my daughter is named for four different families! (44fc)
>
> My birthmother's oldest sister (the only one who knew of her pregnancy) is named Ann Carol. My name is Carol Ann. My aunt goes by Carol, as I do. My birth middle name and my adoptive middle name both are Ann. Before I met my birthmother, I decided to refer to her as Mary. That turned out to be her name! (34fc)
>
> When I was a child and played imaginary games--dress-up and so forth--I changed my name, as all little girls do, to Virginia or Elizabeth. Usually I was Virginia. I found my birthmother nine years ago; her name is Virginia. This is very strange! (12fc)

Finding the frequency of similarities in names is noteworthy. Some were the coincidental choice of adoptive families, and some indicated a pre- and perinatal memory component. Further investigation into the significance and selection of names would be a compelling project. In commenting on a child's development of concrete thinking, Piaget (1930) said:

> Names are, to begin with, situated in objects. They form part of things in the same way as do color and form. Things have always had their names. It has always been sufficient to look at things to know their names. . . . To deform the name is to deform the thing. (p. 243)

It is remarkable that uncanny information about names seems to be transferred to unsuspecting, separated family members. Some names were "known" prior to their objects' being observed. An adoptee's sense of family loss occurs at the concrete operational stage, when cognitive reasoning brings realization of lack of biological connectedness; there are no names for the fantasied parents (D. M. Brodzinsky, 1990). It is interesting to speculate whether the actual learning of names after reunion is one key that permits a person whose development was frozen to resume leaps in psychological growth, filling in deficiencies from the concrete operational stage.

10
Connection by Memory

I explain our synchronicities by the fact that I always sensed I had a connection to my mother. I don't know if she whispered it in my ear, but I somehow knew there wasn't any hostility toward me on her part, and that she didn't want to give me up. I always felt that way as a little child, but I didn't know why. I had a secret journal that I kept writing to her, from about the age of six, letting her know what was going on in my life. I still have it.....my mother died before I could show it to her. (53fc)

PRE- AND PERINATAL ATTACHMENT

The symbiotic wholeness of the pregnant mother and her baby is a union of two living as one. The baby receives everything he needs from the mother: nourishment and protection, in the only world he knows. At the same time, the life of the mother is affected by the attachment (Fromm, 1956), and her emotions may contribute to the personality of the unborn child (Feder, 1980).

In 1958 British psychiatrist John Bowlby published a now famous paper, "The Nature of the Child's Tie to His Mother," suggesting that infants become attached to their mothers, and mothers to their infants, not so much from learning as by instinct. They are programmed from conception to express that attachment at birth, as a direct result of the genetic heritage of the species. His theory upset psychological scholarship of the day, which had rejected the term "instinct" in favor of environmental influences. Bowlby borrowed from the science of ethology (the study of the behavior of organisms living in their natural habitats), whose biological literature showed that strong infant-mother bonds can be formed through mechanisms unrelated to feeding gratification or rewards.

Prior to this, psychiatry and psychology lacked a biological basis, concerned more with individual development and psychopathology. Attachment theorists have now shown that mental disturbance can best be understood against a unifying phylogenetic background. "We must never forget that the actual *experience* of attachment and the symbolic implications of the mother-child relationship reach far beyond mere behavioral systems and the neuro-physiological mechanisms responsible for their control" (Stevens, 1982, p. 13).

Anthony Stevens, a psychiatrist and associate of Bowlby, believes that much of the first year of human life may be regarded as a post-uterine embryonic phase, in which helplessness renders the mother indispensable in a dangerous world. A mother has been prepared to become attached to her baby by the months of waiting for its birth.

> *Her libidinal investment is apparent from the moment of birth. In all species of mammal the mother rapidly learns to recognize her own baby and develops a tenacious proprietorial right to it. If any attempt is made to take the infant away she will display violent hostility. Thus, the frequently expressed anxiety of mothers in maternity wards that their child might get swapped for somebody else's is no neurotic foible: it is probably genetically based. It is an expression of the fundamentally biological nature of the individualized bond.* (Stevens, 1982, p. 86)

Evidence of an **archetypal longing** of mothers and children for each other is exhibited in all mammals and is pathetically demonstrated on those occasions when behavioral scientists attempt to separate them. Only by **deception** or brute force can their tight clinging be broken (Bowlby, 1973; Jensen & Tolman, 1962; Stevens, 1982). Birthmothers in support groups frequently express anger that they were **deceived** into thinking they were doing the best thing by surrendering their children.

Bowlby's (1973) studies of children separated from their mothers in hospitals demonstrated **three phases of response** with application to psychoanalytic theory: **Protest** relates to separation anxiety; **despair** relates to grief and mourning; and **detachment** relates to defense mechanisms. Bowlby posited that attachment theory gives a better explanation of these conditions than does psychoanalysis. Stevens (1982) found this a persuasive suggestion, but "would go further and argue that all these crucial areas of psychopathology can be better understood as *natural consequences of thwarting archetypal intent*' (p. 100).

Nancy Verrier (1987) maintains that when an infant is separated from his mother at a time when he has no verbal skills with which to express the psychic trauma, a **primal wound** results. The child has not yet begun to separate his identity from that of the mother and is still in primal relationship to her. The mother at that stage is actually the child's "self" (Neumann, 1973, p. 13). "This incompleteness is often felt, not only in the genealogical sense of being cut off from one's roots, but in a felt sense of bodily incompleteness" (Verrier, 1987, p. 77). Prenatal studies of fetal hearing and breathing indicate that the child has been sensitized to the mother's breathing rhythms, to which he was intended by nature to have familiar access postnatally (McKenna, 1987). In separation, this bewildering displacement of the birthmother's customary and expected rhythms is intensely felt and remembered by the central nervous system of the child (Cheek, 1986; Verny & Kelly, 1981).

PRE- AND PERINATAL COMMUNICATION AND MEMORY

Prenatal communication has been well documented by research, as summarized by Verny and Kelly (1981): An unborn baby is acutely aware of his mother's thoughts and kinesthetic feelings, and has to tell which are essential and which are not. An Austrian study of maternal-unborn communication used ultrasound to record how quickly a resting child responded when his mother heard a frightening statement. It was thought that while a rise in maternal adrenaline levels could partly account for the babies' active kicking, on another level they were responding to their mothers' distress.

It had been commonly taught that the start of conscious awareness begins between the 28th and 32nd week of gestation. At that point, the brain's neural circuits are as advanced as those of a newborn. Some researchers say that a child can remember from the sixth month on; others argue the brain does not have powers of recall until the eighth month. Still others maintain that memory is holographic, or even that it is cellular from the time of conception. None of them doubt, however, that the unborn child remembers and that he retains those memories (Verny & Kelly, 1981). The stories of these adoptees demonstrate:

> *I love sailboats--am not a great sailor, but take great pleasure in boats. I found out I was conceived on a sailboat in Honolulu Harbor. My mother listened incessantly to Elvis Presley's music while pregnant with me. I always loved Elvis's movies, even though as a teenager in the 1970s, this was definitely un-cool! I watched his old movies on the sly.* (12fc)

> *The only thing I might attribute to prenatal memory is that my mother spent a lot of time around horses and loved them dearly. I had a complete obsession with horses. My adoptive parents had no interest and wouldn't buy me a horse or anything. I worked summers mucking stalls so I could pay for riding lessons.* (5fc)

> *At age 14 I had my first experience skiing, and it was "love at first sight." My adoptive brothers and sisters were not impressed with the sport and did not pursue it. I, however, continued to beg my cousins to take me skiing and by 16 had my own pair of skis. In college I skied with "the boys," because none of my girlfriends skied. My sophomore year I went to Vail, Colorado, on semester break to work and ski. During the winter at school I worked weekends at a ski camp. After graduation I lived and worked at Vail Ski School for a year, then returned to Boston and taught skiing on weekends in New Hampshire and near Boston. As you can see, skiing is a big part of my life. When I got the information on my parents, I found out not only that they were both avid skiers--that's where they met, and my birthmother even worked at a ski area for a time. This was intriguing and also very special for me.* (16fc)

Fetal perception and memory have been investigated by Anthony DeCasper (1980, 1985), professor of psychology at the University of North Carolina in Greensboro. Recent data have given the first reinforced evidence that the unborn child not only hears and recognizes his mother's voice, but also apparently remembers her words. DeCasper worked with women during the last six and one half weeks of their pregnancy, instructing them to read to their unborn children twice a day. Group A read *The Cat in the Hat*, and Group B read *The King, the Mice and the Cheese*. Within a few hours after birth, the researchers offered the babies a choice between the stories, both read by their own mothers on tape. Eleven of the 12 babies showed a preference for the familiar story rather than the new one, by adjusting their sucking rhythm. The study suggested sensitivity to rhythm, intonation, variation in frequency, and the phonetic components of speech. These newborns exhibited a consciousness of their mothers which apparently existed for some time prior to birth.

A related experiment was conducted by Robin Panneton (1985), a student of DeCasper. She found that newborns preferred a familiar melody as opposed to an unfamiliar one; responses were compared to a control group which showed no systematic preference.

Other examples of possible memory influence are these:

I grew up in suburbs of Midwestern cities and always had some unusual interests for a city girl: country music, ranches, rodeos, and cowboys! I now know that my birthmother is a rancher, was in the rodeo club at school, and her four brothers were all rodeo riders. (72fc)

My daughter especially likes the "Hallelujah Chorus." Recently I went through some old school memorabilia and found that I had performed it with a full orchestra and chorus while two months pregnant with her. At the time I first seriously considered searching, my daughter was working at a job she disliked in an insurance office in the state where our separation had taken place. She had moved 1,200 miles to be there, with no conscious intention of reunion. I had worked in an insurance office there during the third through sixth months of my pregnancy. Did she have a prenatal memory of that? Several years later, when my search was nearing completion, she had again taken a job in insurance, this time in another state. Her first telephone call to me was placed from that office. Since our reunion, she is no longer in the insurance business. (36fp)

Out of the new studies has come the realization that human intrauterine bonding is equally as graded and complex as post-birth bonding, which is part of the same vital continuum. A newborn responds naturally to his mother's touch and eye contact because of his intimate, prenatal acquaintance with her, according to Verny and Kelly (1981): "After all, sensing his mother's body and eye language is not very challenging to a creature who has honed his cue-reading skills in utero on the far more difficult task of learning to respond to her mind" (pp. 75-76).

NEGATIVE PRENATAL EXPERIENCE

Not all womb-life is pleasant, and negative imprinting is known to occur. A personal report of intrauterine trauma is that of Australian psychiatrist and primal therapist Graham Farrant (1987), who discovered in confusing, emotional primal sessions the knowledge that his mother had attempted to abort him by taking pills, then getting into a hot bath. When he telephoned his 79-year-old mother, she said it was exactly what happened. "She burst into tears and revealed that I couldn't possibly know that, because she had not even told my father; she never told anybody. But it enabled her and me to develop a relationship" (p. 32).

He is now working on a book to present his ideas of cellular consciousness, and theorizes that the state of consciousness of both parents profoundly affects the gametes, from the time of conception. From his clinical experience with primal therapy and adoption issues, Farrant (1987) remarked, "It's crucial in my experience for an adoptee to find his or her parents--*crucial*. Life is never resolved until you *know* where you came from" (p. 31).

An adoptee's nightmare of prenatal memories was described to me. Included is the element of her adoptive mother's intuitively accurate response:

At age 16 my adoptive daughter, Ann, was having a recurrent dream which was upsetting and depressing her greatly. She stated that the dream was always the same, and she could not understand its meaning or why she kept dreaming it: She felt like she was underwater and hearing people she did not know--a woman's voice, and a man's voice loud with yelling. She said she became afraid each time he yelled. But the strange part was that she could not understand the words, as they were in a foreign language.

My daughter was most disturbed, and I felt I must help her. Immediately, an answer formed in my mind. I had just been reading of research done on babies in utero. "Perhaps you are not underwater, but in your mother's uterus in the amniotic fluid. The voice of the woman is your mother's." Here, Ann interrupted excitedly, "And the man yelling is my father!" *"No, Ann, it is your mother's father, your grandfather."* *Her tears were dried, and she never again dreamed this dream. It was all but forgotten until Ann was 28 years old, and her birthmother found her. She told Ann that her father, Ann's grandfather, was very hard on her, always yelling at her about something. At home, her parents used their native language, German.* (68fo)

Another adoptee was able to understand her phobia by discovering its prenatal origin:

I have always had a fear of bad car wrecks, such as getting broadsided. I have learned that when my mother was seven months pregnant with me, she was in a car accident; the car rolled seven times. Mother had only a scratch. (29fc)

Memories of birth. David B. Chamberlain (1988), who has followed Thomas R. Verny as President of the Pre- and Perinatal Psychology Association of North America, has collected documentary evidence that babies remember their birth experience, based on research of the past 25 years in embryology, neurology, and developmental psychology. His book summarized the most recent discoveries in development from conception to birth, learning and memory processes, and actual reports of birth memories: delivery room experiences; physical body memories of the birth process; and distress in the hospital nursery. In a fascinating phenomenological study of the birth feelings of 13 subjects during psychotherapy, Khamsi (1987) found they "seem not to be discrete, encapsulated feelings simply about birth. When consciously experienced, birth feelings seem inextricably interwoven with prenatal, childhood, and present events" (p. 57).

In his own research, Chamberlain has compared the birth reports of hypnotized children, who had no conscious memories of birth, with reports given by their mothers, who had never spoken about the experiences with their children. The following story confirms Chamberlain's work: In hypnotic regression, a reunited adoptee saw himself as a newborn baby, with a woman he knew to be his mother holding him and smiling down at him. The room was all white, with a white floor and tall windows. The therapist said the young man must have carried the memory all his life at some level. His birthmother was astonished and said to him:

> *I know the moment you are talking about. The nurse had brought you into the room and it was the first time you had your eyes open. And I looked into them and felt the most indescribable delight, like I was saying hello to your soul. And it seemed I had known you forever, and that I could look through your eyes and see heaven. The room had tall windows and a white linoleum floor.* (Schaefer, 1991, p. 284; 62fp)

Recent research in the area of memory has delved into the ways in which information is selected, coded, organized, stored, retrieved, and used. Yet inquiry into anomalies of recognition or recall has been minimal, ranging from Reed's (1988) cognitive explanation of normal psychological processes to Sheldrake's (1981) morphogenetic field hypothesis of a causative state with which the human brain resonates. Following are some of the more imaginative ways to "think about thinking" about memory:

There have been extensive studies on the elusive memory traces, engrams, in the organism (Pribram & Broadbent, 1970). Neurosurgeon Karl Pribram (1984) went further to develop a holographic model of cerebral functioning, suggested that not only memory, but all comprehension and perception of the outside world require decoding from their "frequency domain," an intermediate area between the object and the image in which time and space are collapsed.

Protein synthesis and RNA. Psychiatrist Arnold Buchheimer (1987) also challenged the prevailing assumption that memory is exclusively a function of the brain. Based on empirical observations in regressive-abreactive therapy, as well as the research of psychobiologists, neurophysiologists, and psychologists of the late I960s and early 1970s that linked cellular learning with long-term learning, he proposed that **memory storage exists throughout the body**, and that **memory storage is protein related**. His thinking is that RNA is the memory storage facilitator in cellular protein, and that it is RNA rather than the engram that *stores, accumulates,* and *transmits* memory. What is called an engram is the unobservable electrical phenomenon which serves as a *connector* between perception and storage and between storage and retrieval. If genetic information flows from DNA to RNA to protein (Judson, 1979), "One could almost explain the entire human developmental sequence, à la Piaget or Erikson, with the manufacture and strength of protein synthesis and RNA" (Buchheimer, 1987, p. 57).

It is thought that, in learning, RNA transfers behavior tendencies (Gispen, Perumal, Wilson, & Glassman, 1977) that have been programmed genetically, congenitally (pre- and perinatally), and adventitiously throughout life. As a result, learned events and similar tasks may pervade the entire body. **It is possible for persons to remember very early sensory experiences because they are part of the body's genetic-experiential system and retrievable under psychogenic stimulation.** "Memory is holographic; thus, if cellularly stored, it is represented throughout the entire body" (Buchheimer, 1987, p. 54).

If that is so, then it is not surprising that a mother and child retain memories of each other. In their search for both wholeness and a self, they are internally preoccupied, conscious of being part of a larger whole, and open to synchronicity. Buchheimer commented on work with an adoptee who recovered from schizophrenia after reunion with his birthmother: "Adoptees have a pervasive sense of loss and abandonment. What heals the split is intensive regression" (personal communication, March 11, 1991).

The following anecdote combines the element of an altered state with the reemergence of a memory from a few weeks after birth. It is the personal story of Jean Paton, founder of Orphan Voyage and a pioneer in the adoption rights movement:

> *When I was in therapy a long time ago, I had a kinesthetic dream of sobbing and being patted on the back. I assumed this was a separation trauma. About 15 years later I entered the home of my mother, who was then 69, and I was 47. Only a few minutes after I came into the room with her, she was graphically describing how I had been sobbing in her arms (at the age of two months), and she was patting me on the back! You can imagine how startled I was, and how sure I was from that moment on, if for no other reason, that she was indeed my mother. We continued in relationship for the next 12 years until she died in 1967. We were separated when I was four months old, from the place where I was born and where she lived with me during those months. (You may realize that in that far-ago time there were no baby formulas.)* (40fc)

SYNCHRONICITY AND REUNION

The participants in the next story were also together for a few months before surrender, and memory is a likely factor in the drama:

> *I always felt a piece of the puzzle was missing. It took me a long time to begin my search, and it wasn't until it was over that I understood I had been guided all along. Throughout my life I was always triggered by an interest in sign language, and I learned it from friends and people in my church. When I finally located her, Mom and I exchanged letters and pictures. In one letter she wrote, "For a long time I cried for you. I prayed you were safe. I hoped I would find you again." Then she came to visit me, and we met at the airport. . . . I raised my hands in front of me in a gesture God had been preparing me for without my knowing why. You see, there was something else I had found out: Mom was deaf. We came closer. Carefully, my hands signed the one beautiful word I had longed to express: Mother.* (58fc)

The unconscious representation of a young child surfaced in the following anecdote:

> *I was taken away from my birthmother when I was almost four years old. I was told I was adopted from the beginning, but none of the details except that my birthparents were killed in a car wreck [untrue]. I had no conscious memory of my life before I was adopted--the mind does some strange things, I guess. There was a vague memory of playing near some railroad tracks with a friend when I was small; however, I didn't remember how old I was or how old my friend was, her name, or anything. I asked my adoptive mother, and she said I was never around a track. While I was searching, I went to check out an address my mother had listed as the address where she lived when I was taken away, and found that it was located very near a railroad track. I was shocked. When I contacted my mother, I found out I had told the probation officers that someday I would find my mother, even though they might take me away. **I did.*** (29fc)

Morphic resonance. British biologist and biochemist Rupert Sheldrake (1981) challenged mechanistic science with his idea that the form, development, and behavior of organisms are influenced by morphogenetic fields which show cumulative properties. Through direct connections not reduced by space or time, these fields are molded by the form and behavior of past organisms of the same species in a process he called morphic resonance. DNA is involved in heredity as a tuning mechanism to enable an organism to make its characteristic proteins, then to tune in specifically to memories that are in "the whole of the past" which may be accordioned into the present, "so that the past is present always" (p. 159). Acknowledging that it is only a hypothesis, and urging experimental testing, Sheldrake (1981) said:

> *Our brains may tune in to our memories, but the memories need not be stored inside the brain. If they are not stored inside the brain, other people might be able to tune in to our memories, or we might tune in to other people's memories.* (p. 166)

Is it possible that the adoptee in Chapter 1 could "tune in" to his great-grandparents' memories when selecting their house to buy?

To summarize the findings of the 70 families who contributed to my exploratory study, 17 related one or more anecdotes with a possible memory component (prenatal or preseparation): Four female adoptees "knew" or made coincidental use of their mothers' names, as for imaginary friends. A male adoptee used an older sister's name and the name of his mother's hometown in naming his own daughter. Four adoptees (three male, one female) were drawn to the towns in which they were born. Two female adoptees had fears related to specific prenatal trauma. Two adoptees (one male, one female) experienced very early memories in therapy. Three female adoptees evidenced possible memory of language: French, German, and sign language. Four female adoptees thought hobbies might have a prenatal memory influence: horses, skiing, sailing, and specific music.

11
The Psychic Connection

Psychoanalyst Jan Ehrenwald (1977) believed that telepathy or intuition is involved in more than an incidental manner in the early parent-child relationship, and may be the main feature of the mother-child symbiosis. A human infant is more dependent on its parents than is any other creature. What might seem like a communication void in the early symbiotic phase is made up by the telepathic contact between mother and child. Ehrenwald postulated that there is no psychological gap between them, due to a continued fusion of the neonatal with the maternal ego. Within the single, not yet differentiated personality structure, telepathy follows patterns of intrapsychic communication. **Ehrenwald noted the regressive quality of telepathic interaction, but that spontaneous flashes do occur in later life, particularly between mother and child, when in a crisis situation, or when more sophisticated channels of communication are unavailable.**

These are representative examples in mothers and daughters physically separated since birth:

> *When my daughter was 13 years old, I found myself thinking about her constantly. I felt that if I were with her, things would be different. That is the year I decided that someday, somehow I would find her. I later found out that was the year she lost her virginity to an older man, and she was having great problems with her family.* (59fp)

> *I kept a diary before our reunion, and I documented in this diary the fact that when my daughter was 15 years old, I felt unusually upset over our separation. When we were reunited, she told me she had run away and had tried to find me at age 15, to no avail.* (47fp)
>
> *I have found out my mother died in a car accident; the car went over a cliff. When I was in school I used to sketch **cliffs**.* (30fc)

Cassandra Eason (1990) collected stories of this type from many families after her own son, when less than three years old, "saw" and told her of his father's motorcycle accident as it occurred 40 miles away. In another family, a 10-year-old girl suddenly thought to herself as she watched television, "If my father has had an accident I shall take a small bunch of grapes with a huge red ribbon tied to them to him in hospital" (p. 59); five minutes later she had a call from her crying mother, who was at the hospital just after the father's accident.

Eason (1990) included anecdotes of the innate ability of mothers who knew when an infant or child was in danger and interrupted their activities or covered great distances to reach the child just in time to save his or her life. A health professional she interviewed said that "because these experiences are not well documented or researched and worse still not acknowledged, a valuable warning system for babies' health could be lost" (p. 41). Krippner (1978) said that mother-child telepathic experiences are prime examples of extrasensory perception, or psi, and that they occur at the deepest unconscious levels of human personality.

Both Berthold E. Schwarz (1980) and his mother had premonitions of his brother's death in Germany. In Schwarz's (1971) family study, hundreds of episodes of telepathy occurred most frequently at what seemed to be an intersection of the child's and the parent's emotional needs. "Among other reasons, the emotional necessity of repressing such material of significance to both partners in the telepathic event gives the probably erroneous impression that it is a rare or vestigial oddity" (p. 222). In clinical work Schwarz observed that telepathic instances between himself and clients in therapy occurred more with persons in dissociative states than with other conditions.

For many children the attention deficit and hyperactivity disorder (ADHD; formerly termed ADD) includes a dissociative state, as well as the typical motor hyperactivity, impulsiveness, distractibility, and inability to concentrate for long periods of time. Deutsch et al. (1982) gave the results of a sample from two populations of children diagnosed with ADD. Their data indicated that male adoptees have a 32% to 36% chance of exhibiting ADD symptoms, while the figure for female adoptees was 6% to 14%. In applying all possible variables to these estimates, and if the actual percentage of adoptees in the general population is only 1%, then the ADD rate among adoptees could be closer to 0.510. As a possible explanation, the researchers noted a high rate of alcoholism, hysteria, sociopathy, or psychopathy among the birth relatives of hyperactive adoptees; and also that ADD has a moderate genetic component (Cantwell, 1975).

This area invites further inquiry. Certainly the primal separation from their mothers must be considered as a factor in adopted children with ADHD. A dissociative state may function to enhance their ability to send or receive messages to/from their birth families. Are their antennae out? A brief excerpt from Chapter 9 underscores that question:

> *When I was in preschool I said, "I have a sister, but I don't 'member her name now." It was of sufficient seriousness to warrant a conference and a written report to my adoptive parents, and I have a copy of it. I now know that a sister had been born into my birth family, and they unknowingly gave her my name!* (36fc)

Children often have an active fantasy life. Invisible playmates, fairies, or communication with deceased relatives may be simply imaginary, have still-unexplained psychic components, or serve as a means of coping with stress. A child psychotherapist at the Tavistock Clinic in London, Eileen Orford, commented to Eason (1990), "A gran who has died may be held in memory as someone who is very kind. So when a child is ill or unhappy, it is natural for him to revive the memory of a loving person to care for him" (p. 127). Eason questioned how a child could possibly retain a memory of someone who died before he was born.

Is there genetic memory? What kind of connection remains between separated family members? A young woman reported:

> *In a car accident I heard directions: "Hold onto the wheel!" If I hadn't, I would have been thrown and dragged. I always felt it was my mother yelling that day. (She was deceased before I found the family.)* (48fc)

Children separated from their families may have a special kind of communication for critical events. Psychiatrist Joost A. M. Meerloo (1964) described it:

> *Communication between various forms of organic life is a unification tendency--a search for the lost union and inertia. We may compare it with the principle of "entropy" from physics. Ferenczi explains communication as a danger reaction. Life melts together when something threatening occurs.* (p. 3)

He felt that this principle, although yet unexplained, tentatively connects the relation between severe crisis and the need for increased communication through telepathy. "Man's unconscious still has contact with a four-dimensional, timeless and magic world which we are just beginning to explore with conscious means" (Meerloo, 1964, p. 19).

Louisa E. Rhine, who, with her husband, J. B. Rhine, did some of the pioneering work in extrasensory perception at the Duke University Parapsychology Laboratory, then at their Institute for Parapsychology sponsored by the Foundation for Research on the Nature of Man, wrote about some of the 10,066 case histories she had collected and classified as intuitions, realistic dreams, unrealistic dreams, and (more rarely) hallucinations. Within each of these four forms, an ESP experience was typed as either clairvoyant, telepathic, or precognitive. L. E. Rhine (1967) said it was the form, not the type, that gave clues to the kind of process by which the information made its way to consciousness.

In reports from women to L. E. Rhine, stories about childbirth and finding lost objects were frequent topics. If those are common subjects in women's intuition, they may be expected in mothers traumatically separated from their offspring at birth who long to find them. A mother had no idea she was receiving information about the location of her lost son:

> I had a nervous breakdown, during which time I was very anxiety-ridden about people being taken away in trains from a certain city. It was like a nightmare of something bad happening to my son, except I did not know he was living in that city at the time! (49fp)

A psychoanalytic term for emotional investment, the concentration of psychic energy on some particular person, thing, or idea is **cathexis**. There may be no stronger cathexis than a mother's longing for her lost child, strengthening the possibility of intuitive messages in crisis. One birthmother's recurring nightmares of her daughter's sexual molestation were, sadly, confirmed in detail after their reunion ("Profiles: Search and Reunion," 1989). Schaefer (1991) noticed, "Women separated from their children at birth whom I had met seemed to be extremely telepathic. Each time this concept was discussed within our support groups, it seemed to explain so much of what otherwise seemed unexplainable" (p. 258).

> One day on my morning walk, as my search was nearing its end, I picked up a package of cigarettes that had been tossed on the swale, seemed compelled to take it home, and smoked one on the porch. This was entirely out of character for me! I had smoked neither before nor since and was vehement in my condemnation of the habit. I now strongly believe that through this absurd synchronicity God was preparing me for the fact that the daughter I found was still a smoker (she has since quit), and I could accept her without reservation. (36fp)

No signal or carrier has yet been identified for telepathy and other psi phenomena, and it is not my goal to digress into unanswered questions of right-brain activity or extremely low frequency (ELF) electromagnetic waves. Gatlin (1977) postulated that psi could best be interpreted as meaningful information creation, and "The information involved has not been transmitted, but rather **created** by the mechanism of **synchronicity**" (p. 16). Rollo May (1975) said that an intuitive insight is designed to provide missing information, and it

> never comes hit or miss, but in accordance with a pattern of which one essential element is our own commitment. . . . The idea . . . came in order **to complete an incomplete Gestalt** . . . this unfinished pattern, this unformed form constituted a "call" that was answered by the unconscious. (pp. 65-66)

Reunited families, who may have assumed that their broken Gestalt was connected only at the point of physical reunion, may be surprised to learn that unifying communication passed between them during separation, in an unconscious patching of an incomplete Gestalt. Is it possible that the intuitive call and its response have a genetic tuning mechanism?

From 23 families who gave me their accounts of experiences of accurate DREAMS or INTUITION, the following data emerged:

- 17 were hunches or intuition.
- 8 were dreams.
- 6 were knowledge of crisis.
- 3 daughters knew when their mothers died.
- 10 came through kinesthetic sensation.
- 6 came through internal visual representations.
- 5 were internal auditory knowledge of names or advice.
- 20 were experienced by adults (17 female, 3 male).
- 7 were experienced by children (6 female, 1 male).

Five of the children felt they **knew** they had siblings. One demanded that her adoptive parents adopt a sister for her (and they did), at the same time her birthmother died, and her natural sister was placed in welfare facilities.

> *When I was little, I used to dream of having a big sister who would come and rescue me. I fantasized a lot about it during the day. Now we're reunited, like best friends. It's great. (31fs)*

> *A hunch I always had since I was a small child of eight or nine was that I either had sisters, or I wanted some so badly that I wished I had some in my adoptive family. Instead, I had an adoptive brother four years older-- just like one of my three birth sisters. (19fc)*

I have a brother who was conceived eight months after I was born. We feel close. He says he always imagined he had an older sister. (28fc)

[Although not yet having had a reunion at the time] my son said he "knew" that I and other relatives were in attendance at his high school graduation. And we were. (3fp)

When I was nine years old I demanded a sister from my adoptive parents. They then adopted another girl. I have since found out that my real sister was orphaned at this time. Our mother died, and she had no one and was put into welfare homes. I believe I know the day my mum died, as I had an uncontrollable outburst one day. My anger was extreme, and I nearly killed a friend of mine. All my life I have had times when I sensed things; sometimes I see people or places or dream them, and then later I find myself with these people or in the particular place. (30fc)

The next two astonishing stories are from adopted women who are artists. The unexpected information they received about their mothers' homes came in the form of apparently clairvoyant, detailed visual representations which were expressed by drawing and painting:

Within days of knowing that the agency had found my mother, before I talked to her, even before I received her first letter, I knew that I wanted to paint her something, as well as write to her. I did a painting of a sunroom, kind of a sun porch: there was a wicker chair; a little coffee table with a pot of tea, some teacups, and a tray of cookies; and then a vase of Bird of Paradise flowers in the background. The painting represented what I thought our first meeting might be, that we might sit down together. When my mother received it, she nearly flipped. It was just like her sunroom! She is British and drinks tea constantly; that teapot is out all day every day. And she had just that week received the Bird of Paradise arrangement from a good friend! (70fc)

> *All of my (deceased) mother's colleagues at the university gave a party for me, to tell me their recollections of her, to give me some small items, to meet me, and to talk to me. It was very nice. There was a little five-year-old boy there, and he mistook me for my mother a few times, because we looked a lot alike. He was sitting on my lap, and I was drawing with him. At one point I said, "I'm tired of drawing for you all during this party, so I am just going to draw two more things, and that will be the end of it." He said, "Well, draw me a house." I had only been in Canada for 24 hours at that time. I drew a really weird house. It was very strange, with a garage in the front and two dormers on the top, but the dormers were placed in a strange way. The house had a turquoise garage door, and all the trim was in turquoise.*
>
> *I noticed that everybody was staring at me and didn't talk to me after that. Nobody said anything, and I didn't know why; I just thought that maybe the party had gone on for too long. Next I drew a Snoopy dog. I don't know why; I had never drawn a Snoopy before. My sister asked, "Why did you draw a Snoopy?" I said, "Oh, I don't know. It just popped into my head, and I drew it." Nobody said anything, and the party went on for about another hour.*
>
> *The next day I was given a tour, and we went to the house where my sister and my mother had lived for 12 years. We pulled into the driveway, and it was **exactly** the house I drew! It was even in turquoise. My sister said, "Do you see why no one knew what to say to you? You scared them all; they didn't know what to do. It was too much of an accuracy. You drew exactly this house, and it's a strange house. And now I want to show you one more thing." She took me up into the attic and pulled out a scrapbook; it was to her from our mother. It said "Happy 18th birthday--love, Snoopy," and there was a little Snoopy underneath. She said, "That's why it was so strange that you followed the house right up with a Snoopy!" (53fc)*

These experiences of telepathic, precognitive, and clairvoyant information received through intuition, dreams, hallucination, or sensation, particularly in times of crisis, may begin to answer the **When?** and **How?** of anomalous cognition and communication. **Unusual knowledge was characteristically perceived with certainty and marked in the mind; then it was acted upon, told to a witness, or put on paper.**

TIMES OF CRISIS

Both this young birthmother and birthfather had accurate premonitions that their baby needed them, but fear prevented action. After reunion they learned their son had been in foster homes after relinquishment, then adopted twice, and the last adoptive father died before the adoption was final. Their story is soon to become a movie made for television:

> *Running like an undercurrent through my days was a growing anxiety about my son's welfare. Sometimes I had a dreadful sense that something was wrong with him. And then, as if to compensate, I had a fantasy that I played over and over in my mind, many times a day, every day, that his placement had not worked out. That Sister Dominic would call and ask if we wanted another chance to keep our baby. . . . [The birthfather], with frightening gravity, said he felt something was really wrong with our son. Terror ripped right through me as I heard him voice out loud the awful premonitions I had been having. He wondered if we should call Sister Dominic. I didn't believe she would tell us anything. I was afraid to talk to her.* (Schaefer, 1991, pp. 116-117; 62fp)

The following post-reunion episode confirms the postulates of Ehrenwald (1977), that a spontaneous flash of telepathic interaction may occur: in later life, between mother and child, when in a crisis situation, and when more sophisticated channels of communication are unavailable:

> *I searched for and was reunited with my daughter one day after her 20th birthday. She cut off the relationship after six months of what seemed to be a very good relationship. We have had no further contact. However, I subscribe to her local newspaper to know some of what is happening in her life. On [a specific date, three years later] I sensed that something bad was happening to my daughter. I was terribly depressed and spent the whole day in bed crying. I just couldn't shake the feeling all day. In the evening, when I got out of bed, I said to my husband,* **"Something is happening with her, and no one can tell me differently."** *When her newspaper arrived by mail several days later, I opened it and found she had given birth to twin girls on that particular date. They were born by C-section 10 weeks early and were on ventilators. My daughter had been driven to another hospital by ambulance because of the early births. I confirmed all this by calling the hospital staff.* (47fp)

SYNCHRONICITY AND REUNION

Another story is told by a young woman who had a frightening premonition, not long after their reunion, that her sister's life was threatened. It came to her while sewing, which she described as an in-between, "escape" activity, when she was thinking and daydreaming at the same time:

> My sister was working as a practical nurse for a manic-depressive woman whose husband was a stroke victim and needed around-the-clock attention. I was sewing, when all of a sudden something hit me, and I "freaked out." That's the only way to put it. I was shaking. My sister was in **danger**, and someone was going to kill her. I saw it! I saw her lying on a kitchen floor in a puddle of blood. Needless to say, I panicked. I called her house to see if she had gone to work yet, and she had already left. The nanny at her house didn't know me from Adam. I yelled, "Call her husband! Have him call me. Call her and tell her to get out of there now!" Thank God they listened to me. The next day, the woman totally "lost it" and with a knife threatened the nurse who had taken my sister's place (she was not hurt). On another day last spring, I "knew" something was wrong, so I called. My sister's husband said, "She's at the hospital; she broke her foot." (31fs)

The next anecdote is of a post-reunion synchronous experience in which an unexpected, comforting telephone call was received during a period of deep depression:

> I was asked as a birthmother to speak to a group of adoptive parents about search and reunion. This was part of a mandatory education program conducted by an agency during the one-year probation period. It was the first time I had done this. I found it very difficult to "come out of the closet" with this group. I cried all the way home, reliving all the pain. When I got home that night I longed to talk to someone who would understand. As I reached for the phone to call another birthmother, it rang. It was my daughter calling me. This was unusual, as she usually calls on Sunday nights, and this was a Monday. What made her call that night? It wasn't until months later I realized that it was November 1--the 20th anniversary of her birthfather's death--a date she did not know. (14fp)

The Psychic Connection

The following account is included to show a series of post-reunion precognitions, even when actual contact was seldom:

I searched and found my daughter five years ago. At the present time, we have an ongoing relationship, but we are not close--that being her choice, not mine. Over the past five years, I have had many thoughts and feelings that have been very factual: I had a dream in 1987 that my daughter received a car for her graduation from college. Two weeks later she wrote to say her parents gave her their old car for graduation. Several times, driving home from work, I have suddenly said out loud that there would be a letter or gift from her. When I arrived home, there has always been a letter. Two times there were Christmas gifts. Last Christmas I did not hear from her after the holidays to thank me for the things I had sent. I knew that the silence was due to something with her boyfriend. It turns out that his father died just after Christmas, and her time had been taken up with his loss.

This past May I told several people that when I would see my daughter that month, she would tell me that she had broken up with her boyfriend. I found this information out the day before I was to see her, by phone. Due to the recent breakup, she did not want to see me; so this year I have not seen her. This summer, I knew I would be hearing from her and that she was enrolled in graduate school. I knew it would be at the school where she works. Yes, she did write and stated that she was very busy, due to her choice to get an advanced degree at the college where she works. She said it was a big commitment; it will take her four years. This information I knew in my heart, that she would be there for several more years, and I did share that with several others, prior to her letter. (59fp)

Dreams

In the following instances, meaningful ideas came through dreams. The first one involved reception of information about a name--similar perhaps to other uncanny hunches about names--but unusual in that the information came in a sleeping rather than a waking state:

> *During separation from my daughter and at the beginning of a five-year search, I dreamed that her name was similar to the name Meyer. I dreamed of colorful block letters: there was an M, [a distorted E, angled to the right), then I E R. I thought it meant Meyer, and I even called some Meyers to see if they might be my daughter's adoptive parents. It turned out that her name is Minier, but I never would have imagined such a name! Still, I was amazed at how close my dream had been.* (57fp)

> *The only resemblance I can see between my son and me is that we both love the beach. My son had something growing up that I always wanted-- a house right on the beach. He now has his own condo, which is still in the shore area. Before I found him, I pictured him near the beach, and I even had a dream about a sea wall. The house he lived in when I found him was about 10 miles from the ocean, but several years later the adoptive family inherited a grandmother's summer house and moved there. It is right next to a sea wall. One year ago I dreamed my son said he wanted a gold watch, so I bought him one for Christmas. In a computer message to my husband he said, "Tell her I am fine. I wear the watch all the time."* (11fp)

> *There's a saying in AA that there are no coincidences, but God's way of getting your attention; I don't know. I went to Tufts University as an undergraduate. Neponset Circle is near the back gate. I remember slipping out to a drive-in theater during hell week at the fraternity freshman year, and buying beer and liquor at Kappy's near there. I have had recurring dreams of going by Neponset Circle in a car. I really didn't know the significance of the dream, but I had it on many occasions. I learned after reunion that my birthmother used to go roller skating in Neponset.* (43mc)

In February of 1988, after an especially exciting day of searching for my birthmother, I woke up from a dead sleep and said to my husband, "The 18th--what is significant about the 18th?" After a reminder that we were married on May 18, I forgot about it until I received a call on March 18 from the gentleman with the Nebraska Department of Social Services who was doing my search for me, to let me know that, after 16 months of searching, he had met with my birthmother just that afternoon. (52fc)

The tragic ending to this daughter's series of dreams (also mentioned in Chapter 7) **is that the adoption agency refused to believe her intuition, ignored the requests of both parties to be put in touch with each other, and death intervened:**

In February 1990 I began having dreams that my mother was not well and that she was about to be diagnosed with a serious illness. In March I dreamed that she had been diagnosed with cancer and that she was not going to be living very long. I was trying very hard to find her. I went to the agency in Los Angeles where I was adopted and told them of my recurring dreams, that my mother had cancer and was about to be admitted to a hospital. Even though at that time they had a consent form from her, saying that it was all right for me to look for her and for me to have her name and address, they did not give me that information. They would not give me any information at all: zero. As time went on, I cried, and they said, "You're making an emotional connection that isn't there."

In October 1990 I said to the agency, "I feel like it's too late, that she has died, but I still need to find my family." They said, "Well, we'll try to send a letter there." Later they said, "Oh, it came back, returned. She probably moved and forgot about you."

In January 1991 I got my mother's first name; in March I was able to get her address, because I literally begged for it. I found out that I was exactly right, that she had been diagnosed with cancer in March 1990. The agency's letter had come back because she had moved from the town where she had been teaching to enter the hospital in Montreal. She died in September 1990. **I was correct.** (53fc)

12
Connected by Genetic Architecture

DEVELOPMENTAL BEHAVIOR GENETICS

Behavioral genetics is the field of exploring the etiology of individuality, the differences among individuals in a population. It touches the age-old controversy of nature versus nurture; its approach is empirical and inductive. Further integration of behavioral genetics and developmental psychology has resulted in a still newer interdiscipline called developmental behavioral genetics. Initial research has important implications for developmental psychologists (Plomin, 1986). From this field of inquiry have come reports of particularly uncanny and meaningful coincidences in the lives of adoption-separated twins. Researchers at the University of Minnesota have been surprised to find the pervasiveness of genetic influence in their life patterns. For that reason, this area is a major focus in my examination of possible natural or programmed causes in seemingly acausal events of synchronicity between separated family members. Following is a brief summary of pertinent research:

The three basic methods used in the study of developmental behavioral genetics are family, twin, and adoption studies. In **family** studies, genetically related individuals are compared to examine familial resemblance; this resemblance cannot prove genetic influence, because similar environments could also be a causative factor. Work with **twins** was first suggested by Galton (1875), the father of human behavioral genetics, and it has been done in a number of nations, including Australia, Finland, Sweden, the United Kingdom, and the United States. Fraternal and identical twins are observed for genetic variability, and equal environments are assumed, although recent research would dispute that similarity (Plomin, 1986). Behavioral geneticists (Bouchard, 1984; Cavalli-Sforza, 1975; Kamin, 1981; Lewontin, 1975; Plomin & DeFries, 1985) consider the **adoption** design the most powerful, particularly with **twins reared apart**, because it permits study of the effects of heredity in a randomized family environment. At the same time, genetically unrelated family members living in the same household can be examined for environmental influences.

Eaves, Eysenck, and Martin (1989) pointed out that "the simple equation 'phenotype = genotype + environment' does not do justice to the variety of causes of differences in attitudes and personality" (p. 3). A *phenotype* has been defined as those characteristics of an organism that are expressed and measurable, and a *genotype* as those characteristics that influence the phenotype but are capable of alteration by selective breeding. Deficiencies in classic genetic quantitative models when applied to human behavior have necessitated the development of new models to express, for example, what parent-child correlation to expect from a knowledge of correlations between twins (Eaves et al., 1989), or to test the internal consistency of adoption data and the relative strength of genetic and environmental transmission parameters (Coon, Carey, & Fulker, 1989).

The Colorado Adoption Project. A longitudinal study of the etiology of individual differences in development is led by Robert Plomin at the Institute for Behavioral Genetics, University of Colorado at Boulder. It was formulated by Plomin, director of the study, and John C. DeFries, director of the Institute, in 1974; it is the most extensive study of parent-infant resemblance and difference ever implemented. Nearly 1,000 adoptive and nonadoptive parents are participating.

A sample of 182 adopted infants and 165 matched nonadopted (control) infants was tested in two-and-one-half-hour visits at one and two years of age. As preliminary principles, Plomin and DeFries (1985) found: The etiology of individual differences in motor development and physical growth includes heredity; genes produce change as well as continuity in development; and associations between environmental measures and infant development are often mediated genetically.

Through the cooperation of Lutheran Social Services of Colorado and Denver Catholic Community Services, both the adoptive parents and the birthparents of the adopted children, as well as the nonadoptive control parents, were given a one-time, three-hour battery of behavioral measures. The children will be evaluated at intervals through adolescence to age 16; at that time they will be given the same test taken originally by their parents. The parent-offspring design of the study limits it to finding genetic influence only when certain conditions are met: The measures in both infancy and adulthood must be heritable; and the measure in infancy must be correlated genetically with the measure in adulthood.

Minnesota Study of Twins Reared Apart. Ongoing research which combines twin and adoption designs is that of Thomas Bouchard, Jr., and the Minnesota Study of Twins Reared Apart. It is a section of the Minnesota Center for Twin and Adoption Research at the University of Minnesota, where Bouchard is Chairman of the Psychology Department. A primary objective of this team is to study the relationship of: (a) differences in medical and social life histories, and (b) current medical and psychological differences between twins who were separated very early in life, reared apart during their formative years, and reunited as adults.

Since 1979, over 100 sets of reared-apart "identical" or monozygotic (MZA) and "fraternal" or dizygotic twins (DZA) or triplets have undergone approximately 50 hours of psychological and medical assessment including: a 20-part blood analysis, two mental ability batteries, four personality trait inventories, and three occupational interest inventories. Separate examiners conduct interviews for such aspects as IQ, psychiatric evaluation, life history, and sexual history. The twins' rearing environments are systematically assessed, and they complete independent questionnaires under supervision (Bouchard, Lykken, McGue, Segal, & Tellegen, 1990). Subjects have been primarily from the United States and the United Kingdom, with some also from Australia, Canada, China, New Zealand, Sweden, and West Germany.

Although the researchers set out to identify differences in behavior shaped by environmental influences, it was the frequency of uncanny similarities they found most remarkable. The following descriptions from the Minnesota study are included here to show their resemblance to the categories found by reunited adoptees and their parents:

The Minnesota project began when Bouchard heard of monozygotic twins separated at birth, raised by adoptive families 45 miles apart, and reunited in 1979 at the age of 39. He recognized it as a rare scientific opportunity for a quite definitive and pure method of separating the effects of heredity and environment, and he contacted them immediately. Coincidentally, both had been named James, and they have become known as the "Jim twins."

Beyond that first surprise, an unlikely **chain of coincidences** soon became apparent in their life histories. Both had married and divorced women named Linda and remarried women named Betty. They named their sons James Allan and James Alan. Both had once owned dogs named Toy. Each had law enforcement training and worked part time as a deputy sheriff. They made similar items in remarkably parallel workshops. They drove Chevrolets and had vacationed at the same three-block-long beach in Florida. Both liked stock-car racing and disliked baseball, chain-smoked the same brand of cigarettes, and chewed their fingernails. In different cities, each lived in the only house on his block with a white bench around a tree in the front yard.

More understandably, the medical histories of the Jim twins showed parallels: In similar deep, drawling voices, they used the same words to describe their headache syndrome, which had first occurred at age 18; they had identical pulse, blood pressure, and sleep patterns; they had both gone through what they thought were heart attacks, resulting in diagnosis of no heart disease; and they had gained 10 pounds at the same time. Feeling they had known each other all their lives but had been gone for a long time, they regard their reunion as an almost mystical turning point (Jackson, 1980).

Other twins in the Minnesota study exhibited similarities in names, places, handwriting, grooming, gift selection, purchases, food preferences, idiosyncrasies, habits, phobias, and compulsions. There was a pair of British identical twins, Bridget and Dorothy, who had been raised apart and met for the first time when they arrived at the University of Minnesota for their interviews. Each wore seven rings on manicured hands, a watch and a bracelet on one wrist, and two bracelets on the other (Holden, 1980).

This interwoven fabric of medical and behavioral similarities reappeared so often in the twin studies that Bouchard, who was trained as an environmentalist, remarked early in the project that "the genetic effect pervades the entire structure of personality. If someone had come to me with results like this I wouldn't have believed him. I was aghast" (Jackson, 1980, p. 53).

It is evident that adoptive parents do not acquire a *tabula rasa* when they christen a baby with a new name and obtain an altered birth certificate. The narratives of reunited parents and children contained in this book exhibit similar categories of coincidences, but not in the quantity that identical genomes apparently cause for twins. A female adoptee said:

> *These are the things my birthmother and I have in common: We both laugh alike, use some of the same phrases, and hum when we work. We were both cheerleaders in high school. We were both crowned homecoming queen our senior year. When I was 18 I wore my hair the same way that she did at the same age; we were identical at that age. As I've grown older, I look more like my father. My mother started out majoring in sociology in college and then changed to education; I started out in education and ended up in sociology.* (4fc)

Data from the Minnesota study have led to two general conclusions regarding the sources of behavioral and psychological differences between people: (a) "Genetic factors exert a pronounced and pervasive influence on behavioral variability"; and (b) "the effect of being reared in the same home is negligible for many psychological traits" (Bouchard et al., 1990, p. 223). These statements, while accepted by behavioral geneticists who have come to similar conclusions (Eaves et al., 1989; Plomin & Daniels, 1987), are a distinct challenge to current psychological theories on the etiology of differences in personality, social attitudes, abilities, and interests (Bouchard, 1984; Segal, Grove, & Bouchard, in press).

Their findings support those of many other twin, adoption, and family studies, leading to the generalization that: **"For almost every behavioral trait so far investigated, from reaction time to religiosity, an important fraction of the variation among people turns out to be associated with genetic variation"** (Bouchard et al., 1990, p. 227). Tellegen et al. (1988), in the assessment of twins reared together as well as twins reared apart, found an average of 50% of measured **personality diversity** could be attributed to genetic diversity; the remaining 50% was technically classified as environmental, although improvement was needed in the consistency and stability of a trait scale. "It seems reasonable, therefore, to conclude that personality differences are more influenced by genetic diversity than they are by environmental diversity" (p. 1036). Tellegen stressed that the significance is that heritabilities were found at all, and that they all range about 50%.

The Minnesota twin studies have indicated that two thirds of the observed **variance of IQ** can be traced to genetic variation, at least in the current middle-class environments of industrialized societies (Bouchard et al., 1990). The surprising similarity of MZA adult twins in their social attitudes, such as **religiosity and traditionalism**, has shown that in most families the adoptive parents tend to be less effective, or less inclined to do so, in reproducing their own distinctive imprints (Waller, Kojetin, Bouchard, Lykken, & Tellegen, 1990). A case from my investigation confirms this finding:

> *In my adoptive family there are no preachers, no one in the ministry. In my natural family I found out that two of my great grandfathers (one on my dad's side, and one on my mother's side) were Baptist preachers, just as I am. (56mc)*

In another twin study, Rose and Ditto (1983) found the fear of one's own death and the fear of the death of a loved one were influenced by genetic factors, with increasing monozygotic twin resemblance and decreasing dizygotic twin resemblance over the age of 20. "To our knowledge, it provides the first demonstration of significant changes in heritability across age in social behaviors or attitudes" (p. 367). **Fear of death was also mentioned by an adoptee who was reunited with her birthfather:**

> My father and I are identical in our old-fashioned values, but neither one of us is religious or attended church past the age of 12. We both have a tremendous fear of death; we are very, very terrified of it. We want to stay in the here and now, and we never want to die. (23fc)

Life-course guidance of the genome. The twin studies also suggested that the identical genomes of MZA twins make it likely that their effective environments are similar, reinforcing similar psychological traits. Although the specific mechanisms are largely unknown, it is conjectured that there is an indirect but critical mechanism by which genetic differences in human behavior are expressed in phenotypic differences (Lumsden & Wilson, 1981). **MZA twins, with similar temperaments, may elicit similar parenting responses in their separate adoptive families.** As children and adolescents, they seek similar congenial environments (gene-environment covariance). As individuals they will attend or respond differently or similarly to the same objective experience (gene-environment interaction).

Throughout life, it is genetic individuality that helps guide a person's development in behavior, mobility, learning, and choices. Bouchard et al. (1990) agreed with environmentalist theory that most psychological variance probably has the proximal cause of learning through experience. "The effective experiences, however, to an important extent are self-selected, and that selection is guided by the steady pressure of the genome (a more distal cause)" (p. 227).

Looking into the histories of some of the MZA twins is a quick way to grasp the concept of the steady, life-course guidance of the genome. Genetic influences kick in at different times, as though on cue; photographs and medical records of the reared-apart twins show that change is synchronized. MZA twins not only have similar immune systems (an average of seven out of nine key antibodies in common) and almost identical cardiac and pulmonary histories, but very close timing of the onset of disease (Rosen, 1987).

Developmental Molecular Genetics

New knowledge from the field of molecular genetics has strengthened the base for future research in developmental behavioral genetics. How gene regulation works, with some genes affecting the activity of others, in the development of human life from a single cell to a complex differentiated organism with trillions of cells carrying the same DNA, is a central question.

Timing is an issue unique to development. Certain temporal genes have been found to operate at a distance from structural genes, indicating an unknown mechanism of molecular timekeeping and signaling. Paigen (1980) suggested that "genetic programming is at least an appreciable aspect of developmental regulation and quite possibly the major driving force" (p. 423). A **cassette model** of coordinate gene expression was developed by Herskowitz et al. (1980), in which transposable genes produce genetic rearrangement. Like cassettes in a tape player, when one is completed, it initiates the playing of another.

The cassette model was criticized as being too reductionistic, but in 1984 it acquired renewed interest with the discovery of **homeoboxes**, DNA segments with about 180 base pairs that show up in several gene complexes significant to developmental timing (Gehring, 1985.) "Although the several homeoboxes in the genome might be independent, it is possible that they are cassette duplicates inserted from a master cassette" (Plomin, 1986, p. 40). Provocative parts of the puzzle are inherent in these coincidences, from the same woman who shares with her father a strong fear of death:

> *When my dad first walked through the door, I thought, Oh, my God, it's **me**! I feel like he has been in life all my life. We look alike and are fairly short; we stand alike. We like the same music and food. We both pronounce "sure" as "shore," even though we were raised in different areas. We have a penchant for drag racing and stock cars. We are car fanatics and will buy only GM cars, especially Chevrolet. He despises the color yellow as much as I do; everyone knows that about us.* (23fc)

Connected by Genetic Architecture

SURPRISING GENETIC ARCHITECTURE

Of the original 70 reunited families in my study, half (35) reported surprising, meaningful coincidences that fell into the following categories. Some participants are represented in more than one section, according to the information they provided.

Occupation. Fifteen reunited families were amazed to find similarities in occupational choice; some were between parent and child, and some were between siblings. No one seemed more surprised than the woman who found that both she and her mother had operated housekeeping businesses for most of their adult life, although they were culturally different; the mother was an alcoholic, and the daughter did not drink at all. Another mother-daughter pair had "pumped petrol." Teachers, typists, mechanics, and nurses might seem to be common, likely matches, but they were nonetheless discovered as emotionally significant roles.

Undoubtedly a uniquely meaningful association was that found by the adoptee who shared with a deceased grandfather a zeal and dedication in long-term employment with the American Red Cross. Similarly, an adoptee found that both she and her deceased mother had been active in the work of Amnesty International, beginning at the same time. The father who discovered that his daughter is employed in the film business, as he is, was doubly surprised to learn she lives just five blocks from him. There were also the searching mother and daughter who lived in the same neighborhood and worked in the same store for six months before discovering their relationship.

Reunited families wonder if occupational choice has been: the result of chance; the influence of peers, teachers, and adoptive parents; or determined by genetic traits, genetic memory, and pre- and perinatal impressions. Coincidences in occupation include the following:

> *The most interesting coincidence I have found was that my birth grandfather on my mother's side was involved with the American Red Cross, first in the Army and then afterwards as Development Director and then Executive Director of an area. By the time I found this out, I had been involved with the Red Cross myself for at least six years on many levels, including being an instructor for many different classes. When I*

first became involved with the Red Cross, I found myself very committed to the organization, with a zeal that seemed strange. While I find it a wonderful connection to my family, I feel like the connection also renews my commitment to the organization. (2fc)

Although I seem to be more intelligent and so much unlike my mother (she has an alcohol problem and I do not drink at all), I am very surprised that both she and I have had housekeeping businesses for most of our adult life. (23fc)

I could not have known of this, but I followed in my mother's footsteps exactly. We both pumped petrol. I was always drawn to petrol stations. I also wanted to train as a barmaid, but my adoptive parents forbade me. I found out my mother was a barmaid. (30fc)

My mother became a secretary and excellent typist. She was given awards for her service in the CIA and Navy over a 25-year period. I worked at one point as a secretary and was always considered a good typist. (42fc)

My mother and I are known for our office management skills. Both of us, as well as my brother, a grandmother, and a great-uncle, have worked in insurance offices. (36fc)

My husband's adoptive father is a mechanic. My husband is mechanical and works on an oil rig; so did his birthfather. His birth grandfather owned an auto repair shop. (55fo)

My full brother, half sister, and I are all teachers. Within our teaching profession, both my brother and I work with teaching children about computers. (19fc)

My birth grandmother on my mother's side became a practical nurse after her divorce and worked in the nursery at the hospital where I had been born. I too am a practical nurse and worked in a hospital nursery to put my husband through school. My birthfather has a sister and a niece who are nurses too, which I thought was interesting. (44fc)

Physical idiosyncrasies. Unusual physical characteristics were mentioned as surprising bonds for 14 families. These ranged from weight patterns to nervous habits, posture, beards, a trans-generational bump on the ear lobe, and identical injuries.

> *In talking with Dad, he happened to mention his mother is constantly with a pen in hand, writing words from the conversation. He was stunned to see I do the same thing; it's automatic. His sister has a daughter about my age. When he saw a picture of me as a teenager, he asked me where I got the picture, thinking it was this cousin. He said, "You look so much like your cousin, anyone would think you were twins." He also told me many times how exactly I look like his sister, and if I had seen that woman without meeting my mother, I would assume that she was my mother. He found that rather unbelievable, that I could look like his niece and his sister at the same time. We have the same green eyes and straight hair. And we all have a very unusual bump on our ear! It's like doing a mirror image: Mine is on my left; my dad's is on his right; my son's is on his right; and my aunt's is on her right. So it went from my dad to me to my son, switching back for each generation. (23fc)*

Religiosity. Speculation as to the confounding effects of genetic heritage on religious and cultural preferences might be made. Finding similar values and beliefs in newly reunited relatives was highly meaningful to 11 families. Two adoptees had evidenced an unusual affinity for their Jewish heritage. A Baptist preacher was delighted to find he had followed two great-grandfathers (one paternal and one maternal) into the ministry. He recently reported the joy of baptizing both his mother and his stepfather (56mc). A father and daughter shared a similar intense fear of death. A father and son had each been heavily on drugs before going on a spiritual search.

> *When my son was 13, I thought so much about his having a Bar Mitzvah. I've learned that he was so driven, he did it all himself; his adoptive mother was unable to help. (35fp)*

My daughter's father is Jewish, but I waited to tell her, because her adoptive parents were very strict Catholics. I have a sister that has converted to Judaism; she's married and I have four Jewish nieces and nephews. So finally one day I thought, I think it's time; I'm going to tell my daughter. I did, and she said, "Oh, I knew it, I knew it!" The only friend she ever had in college, was just crazy about, and felt an affinity with, was Jewish. "Oh, I'm so happy! My best friend will be so happy! I can't wait to tell her!" (32fp)

I was placed through a Jewish agency (the first adoption the agency handled) and raised Jewish. I found my birthmother is Catholic, not Jewish as the files said. I was born on Christmas day. My first wife was a Christian. (63mc)

My husband is a birthfather and a pastor. When we found his son, we discovered that both of them had been dope pushers and had exactly the same scenario of being on drugs before going on a spiritual search. Before finding him, we were given the verse from Isaiah 9:6: "Unto us a child is born, unto us a son is given." (26fo)

My mother and I were both raised Baptist--she in the South and I in New York. But as far as convictions that we have now, we believe there is a God and in that basic philosophy, but we're not diehard denominationalists; we do not go to church. (5fc)

My sister was raised Catholic, and I was raised basically a heathen. We did not have religion in my home. Any religion that I had, I had to go out and find. We both became pretty much just Christians. We have the same beliefs as to who God is, and how to instill them in our children; our parenting styles are similar. (31fs)

My father and I are very peace-loving people and believe in helping our fellow man at all costs. We are very much into helping animals and preserving wildlife. I was brought up in the Baptist church, and he was brought up in the Congregational church, but neither one of us attended past the age of 12. My father's father believed that once you die, you die, and that there is no hereafter or soul. My father and I don't necessarily believe that's so; we **don't know**. We both have a tremendous fear of death. (23fc)

I am more of a spiritual person and less of an organized religion person. I think that has to do with the Catholic adoption and the way I was lied to throughout the whole thing. I have been told that my mother was exactly the same. It is so shattering to find out that we were looking so hard for each other, and that somebody was holding the keys for us; they were **our** keys, and they didn't let us use them. That's a very frustrating feeling. And they can't give me her life back; she has died now. I would have respected them more if they had said, "Well, this is just our policy; we know it's unfair." But the lies that I heard! (53fc)

Following is an example of the later discovery of lies told at the time of relinquishment, a past practice of social workers who "played God" in the placement of desirable infants. It seems there was divine intervention after all:

God's presence and my faith were what gave me strength at a difficult time, so my primary request to the social worker was that my baby must be placed with Bible-believing Christians, preferably Baptists. Several weeks later she wrote to me, specifically mentioning their denomination; I noted regretfully to myself that it was not Baptist, but that it was acceptable. After reunion, I learned that it was not true at all. The father had not attended church since childhood, and the mother was a non-practicing daughter of Orthodox Jewish parents.

Faith in a living God was not taught in my daughter's adoptive home; holidays were celebrated in a secular fashion. I am amazed that as a young person she developed her own written moral system, which includes the Ten Commandments and the individual and community values of Thomas Jefferson and Benjamin Franklin, and that she believes in God. She is now dating a Baptist gentleman!

It was a surprise for the adoptive mother to learn that 10 years before finding them, I had become fluent in Hebrew, that I teach the language, lead tour groups to Israel and feel at home there, and am active in Jewish-Christian relations. Now that the adoptive mother has died, I feel a strong, loving connection to her Jewish parents (also deceased), who were my daughter's grandparents, and who had lived on a street with my maiden name. I think they would be pleased to know there remains *someone (albeit a Christian) to say the Kaddish prayer for their daughter, who had left the practice of their faith and had no biological children. Again this year I had expected to say the Kaddish for my daughter's other mom in my home on the anniversary of her death, but by "coincidence" was invited to attend a synagogue service that week, so I stood publicly for the recitation.* (36fp)

Education. Similarities in both IQ and educational choice were involved in the factors mentioned by eight families. Amusing but meaningful to one pair was that the mother started out majoring in sociology in college, then changed to education: the daughter started out in education, but ended up in sociology. Other coincidences evoke a number of causal or acausal explanations:

I fought so hard when I was 13 to take French. I was living in California, and my adoptive family wanted me to take Spanish. That was one of my first really bad disagreements with them. I was very obstinate and said, "I am going to take French! I will run away from home if I can't take French!" I always talked of going to "the Sorbonne, the Sorbonne, the Sorbonne!" Later, I actually spent some time with a friend who was attending there; and in 1988 I visited France at a period when I was becoming very frustrated in my search for my mother, and no one was helping me. She died in 1990; I reached the family in 1991 and learned:

My mother's childhood had been spent in France; she lived there 14 years. After my birth in California, she went back to Canada. She couldn't handle living there any more, so she went to the Sorbonne for two years, learning a new immersion method of teaching language. She then taught French for 20 years in Canada; she was teaching, of course, at the time I first wanted to learn the language. I always wanted to be a teacher. I always taught everyone in the neighborhood to roller-skate; I was always giving "lessons" of some kind. (53fc)

My teenage daughter studied and speaks Russian, and planned to travel to Russia (later discovered as a source of our ancestry). (41fc)

> My mother and I attended colleges just ten miles apart (at different times). I had gone out of state to my college, which was just 70 miles from my mother's home. Neither of us completed our degrees. (18fc)

> My father and I both finished high school and had just a small amount of college, preferring to go out and work rather than continue our schooling. Now, of course, I'm kicking myself and would like to go back. We both tested at 140 in IQ. I used to say to him the expression, "Sometimes I get weirded out," meaning I can get extremely philosophical. I had a hard time explaining it until he said, "Don't feel badly, because my brother gets weirded out on occasion the same way that you do!" We start to think What is earth? or What is a person? My uncle's IQ is 150. (23fc)

> Neither my mother nor I are college-educated. We pretty much made our way on our own. We didn't go off for further education. But we both married very intelligent, bright, smart, college men! (5fc)

> My full sister and I were in the same schools at the same time. We never knew each other but had several of the same friends. We also are alike in many ways--philosophies, hobbies, etc. (51fc)

> Two of my birth sisters went to the same high school as my adopted brother. (19fc)

> My son's experiences in high school were so similar to mine. It is like looking on my counterpart--like a male counterpart. (10fp)

Grooming. Surprises mentioned by eight families included identical selection in jewelry, clothing fashion and colors, hairstyles, and cosmetics.

> A strange coincidence was how we were dressed at the reunion. My outfit was black and white, and my daughter was wearing black and yellow. We both had 30-inch black necklaces and had the same color nail polish by the same company. Meeting my daughter was like looking at myself almost 30 years back. (15fp)

*One year I absolutely **had** to buy a particular short, dark green, corduroy jacket with a hood. It also came in burgundy. I have learned that in the **same year** my daughter **insisted** that she must have the same burgundy jacket, even though her folks were poor. We both had acted entirely out of our normal patterns, with a frantic desire to have that coat. After our reunion, when I was giving my daughter some of my old clothes, she squealed to see the same jacket. (61fp)*

My mother and I wear our hair in exactly the same style and have many of the same mannerisms. She, my two half sisters, my grandmother, and I all use Oil of Olay! (33fc)

We always seem to wear the same color when we meet. The first day we met, we were both wearing black and white with a splash of pink. This year we both seem to have lots of turquoise-colored clothes in our wardrobe. We have some of the same food likes and dislikes. When we talk on the telephone, it's like speaking to myself; our voices are the same. (12fc)

Mating patterns. Eight persons told of a variety of similarities in courtship and marriage patterns, particularly between mothers and daughters. In one instance, each had married and divorced men with the same name who had alcohol problems. In another, each married first-generation Polish men. Another mother and daughter had each married young and lost a child through divorce. Again similar names appear.

My daughter and I both married men by the name of Ken who had alcohol problems--and we've both divorced them! (37fp)

My birthmother married a first-generation Polish man (I hesitate at calling him a gentleman). I also married a first-generation Polish gentleman (no hesitation whatsoever). (42fc)

My life has been similar to my mother's. Both of us married young and "lost" a child in divorce. We had the same jobs and many of the same interests. We both had mental problems and were alcoholics. (48fc)

Broken marriages run in my birth family. My maternal grandmother, birthmother, birthfather, and two sisters all married twice. My brother and I have never married. (19fc)

It has come to light that in 1975 while my sister was on her honeymoon, I met the man I married. Her first husband and my first husband were both truck drivers. Her first husband's name is the same as my current husband's name. She divorced within a year; I tried to leave mine within a year, but it was an abusive relationship. She married again in 1985, which is when I met my current husband. I knew this was the man I was going to spend the rest of my life with. Our husbands are similar: very honest, caring individuals who are willing to take responsibility for their families-- all-around good guys. Her husband plays baseball; mine plays basketball. (31fs)

Collecting and orderliness. Six families were surprised to discover that characteristics heretofore thought to be learned might have a genetic component. Traits of housekeeping and being a "pack rat" came up, as did collecting specific memorabilia, purchasing identical items, or treasuring a particular book.

[The husband of an adoptee relates]: Let me tell you about her adoptive family: Their house is always neat as a pin; a place for everything and everything in its place; if there is no place for it, they throw it away. But my wife is a pack rat--doesn't throw anything away. If there's a flat surface in our house, there's something piled on it. I always thought this had something to do with being adopted, in terms of some sort of insecurity, but the day I walked into her birthmother's house, I was just amazed. Every single flat surface had something stacked on it! I don't mean dirty, but cluttered. Nothing had ever been thrown away. You don't think of "housekeeping" as being an inherited trait, but apparently it is. Now I really believe there must be some sort of "pack rat personality" that is a genetic character trait. It really surprised me. [The adoptee goes on to say]: Don't give either of us flour in the kitchen; we both make a mess. Don't ask us to make biscuits! (44mo,fc)

I recently visited my mother's best friend, who is now living in the house where my mother lived for the last five years of her life. As I was packing to leave, she said, "I want to give you a book; this is a book that your mother loved so much." She went upstairs to get it. At that moment I put into my suitcase the only book that I brought with me, a book that comforts me, **Letters to a Young Poet** *by Rainer M. Rilke (in English). Then the friend came down and said, "This is for you." I unwrapped it, and it was* **Letters to a Young Poet** *in French. (53fc)*

My mother had twin boys, and I had twin girls. We have the same temperament and have similar tastes in country crafts, sewing, and quilting. We enjoy the outdoors and gardening. We hit it off just like we had been doing things together all along. About the time of my last visit to my mother, I had bought a craft book and thought of taking it to her but decided not to; perhaps I would save it for her Christmas gift. When I got to her house, I found she had already ordered and received the identical book! (18fc)

Not long ago, I picked out a puppy. When I later met my mother, I learned it is the same kind of dog she had for many years, a Lhasa Apso. Then I thought of getting another dog, a Pug, which she says is the kind of dog she had after her Lhasa Apso died! (33fc)

Although raised apart, both our daughters not only have the same name, but drew horses, learned sign language, French, flute, guitar, and horsemanship. They always thought of being veterinarians. Both are neat housekeepers, have the same fine hair, degree of nearsightedness, and a good sense of humor. We notice that the reunited daughter uses some of the same idiosyncratic slang phrases, facial movements, and gestures as her birthfather; various things she does remind us fleetingly of other family members. Her weight and dieting patterns are like mine. We both are excessive savers of books, files, and clothes. (36fp)

Handwriting. Six families found similar handwriting: five between a mother and child; one with identical twins; and an additional instance in a child and a paternal aunt.

As a teenager, being very insecure about my physical appearance, I realized that I didn't look anything like my adoptive family. I would wonder what my natural mother looked like. Was she be big-boned and tall like me? Was she shy or outgoing? Sometimes I would try to figure out why I had certain feelings of insecurity about myself. As it turns out, this lady I now call Mom really did have my build, similar hands, feet, and leg problems. We even think along the same lines and have similar handwriting. I feel it is a miracle to come across people who actually are much like myself. I really missed having that "special intuitive connection" to my family that I grew up with. (7fc)

My son and I are very similar, including our handwriting. (49fp)

My daughter and I share printing that is exactly the same; you cannot tell our printing apart, although our cursive handwriting is different. Also, we both have endometriosis. (1fp)

My identical twin sister and I have the same handwriting, which surprised us, for we did not go to school together. We both sit the same way, crossing our legs under us on the chair. A news reporter once said she felt like she was sitting between two bookends! We're like our mother in many ways too. (67fc)

My brother's handwriting is exactly like our mother's; mine is exactly like my paternal aunt's. My birthfather and I both took piano lessons for six years, playing on an amateur level. (42fc)

Voice. Similar voices (usually noticed first by telephone) were mentioned in four parent-child accounts.

When the person who was helping me made a "survey" phone call asking for the adoptive mother, she called me back and said, "Oh, I knew it was your daughter who answered the phone, because she sounded exactly like you!" Our voices are more the same than my other daughter's. (32fp)

While the preceding classes were those most frequently mentioned, other distinctive preferences shared by parents and their children who had no normal sensory contact during the years of their separation included: unusual foods, music, colors, phrases, foreign languages, sports, hobbies, and the writing of limericks:

> *I met my mother in April 1988. During our conversation I mentioned that I wrote limericks. She does too! I went on to tell her that when my son and daughter-in-law had recently adopted twins, they asked me to write a limerick for their birth announcement. My birthmother had adopted a daughter many years after placing me for adoption. She pulled out the birth announcement they had sent at that time--and, yes, it was in limerick form!* (52fc)

> *My mother and I enjoy writing. We are 500 pages into a book about our experiences; it will soon be published. My three half sisters and I all like to eat the skin off the turkey; we are all artistic and good with words.* (56mc)

> *My daughter and I both like to write. I went back to college and took a creative writing course when I was 50. My daughter just wrote a lot of very sad things.* (32fp)

The following stories have special application to birthfather-adoptee similarities:

> *Before contacting my son, I thought I would make a telephone call on a pay phone to the fraternity house, just to see if he was indeed a student there. I was using the cover story of being an old family friend. Of all things, he answered the phone! He had moved off campus, and it was his personal phone number. I almost gasped, because he sounded exactly like his birthfather, a voice I had not heard in 21 years, but would never forget. When we first met, I was amazed, because I hadn't anticipated that he would look so much like his birthfather. During our conversation, whenever he was puzzled about something, he would lean forward on his elbow and pull at his eyebrow. This was a habit that his birthfather had!* (65fp)

I have had several conversations with my son's adoptive mother, in which she confirmed his resemblance to his birthfather. I would begin a sentence about the birthfather, and she could finish it correctly, based on her knowledge of the son! They are both stubborn, moody, tend to be depressed, and drink too much. On the bright side, both are hard workers and have a weird sense of humor. He taught himself to play guitar, and his father taught himself to play the violin. I had one phone conversation with my son last fall, the first direct contact in over five years, and in some ways it was identical to talking to his father years ago. The emotional tone was the same, and he even used some of the same phrases his father had used. I was crying, and he was cold and rational--it was just like old times. (11fp)

My birthfather and I shared a similar trauma at the age of 11. His mother died, and he was adopted by an uncle and aunt that he despised. They split the family up and he was separated from his brothers. It was a very traumatic time in his life. When I was 11, I was told that I was adopted. It was just devastating. I was definitely too old to be told, and probably they shouldn't have even bothered telling me at that point. I wasn't raised with the idea that I was adopted. It was just one day, "Hi. Guess what? You were adopted. Your birthmother's dead [untrue]; you have no family. And we're it." It was like, whooh! I blanked out a lot of what happened to me in my early childhood because of that time in my life. (5fc)

My father and I had not been together for 20 years, but our mannerisms are just alike. We sit alike; we stand alike; when we talk, we use our hands exactly the same. We like the same things; we don't like the same things. We both like to read and write. I even look like him. I have Mom's eyes and her thickness of hair, but I have Daddy's color of hair, and everything else seems to be like him. (64fc)

We discovered my husband has a half brother on his father's side. They have the same kind of physical build. They are both going bald (he gets that from both sides); they both have beards and mustaches; and they both smoke. They drive the same make of pickup and have the same hobbies: fishing, camping, etc. My husband, who was raised in a very rambunctious household, was and is a very quiet person. He gets that from his birthmother; her family is all pretty quiet and relaxed about things. We have three children. The oldest is an artist, and the middle child is musically inclined; these traits came from the birthfather's side. (55fo)

The next few comparisons reflect further parallels among reunited siblings:

I found that one of my sisters had the same towels and dishes as mine. (48fc)

*My sister and I like the same colors for clothing and our homes. Neither one of us fell into the fads that come and go. We both like what we call "classic" clothes that can go from style to style. We both wear a lot of black for evening wear. Black, red, and white are our basic wardrobe colors. We both like to be **very** dressed up, or in real knockaround clothes. We don't have a middle there. We both had long hair and got it cut around the same time. We both liked waitress work, to make a lot of money in a short time, without being committed to it. I learned that once, when I was in the hospital recovering from flu, my sister was also very sick at the same time; they couldn't find anything wrong with her. Since our reunion, we can be talking in a group of people and all of a sudden say the same thing to the same person! (31fs)*

All of the family (I have three full siblings and a half sister) are very big eaters and lovers of food; none of us, luckily, has a weight problem. My maternal grandmother and I have special likes in food: pickled onions, dried apricots, fish, bacon sandwiches, licorice, almonds, and cashews. My brother and I hate eggs of any variety. None of us smoke, and none of the children drink tea or coffee. My mother, two sisters, and I all have a preference for having pet dogs and a distinct dislike for cats. We all have a joy to share and play music (accordion, guitar, keyboards). My mother, a sister, and I share the love of John Denver's music. In 1988 we all went to his concert. On the same day my sister and I both gave our mother John Denver tickets for a Mother's Day present. We were unaware that the other was contemplating this--a prime example of synchronicity. The three of us all played hockey and like to cycle, as does my brother. (19fc)

Connected by Genetic Architecture

A mother found that her reunited sons not only collected identical memorabilia, but had the same football injury and jersey number:

*I have two other children that I subsequently raised. The one closest in age to my reunited son is also a boy, and they are two years apart. It was interesting to find out that both of them had played football, and they had the same jersey number! They had both sustained a football injury, dislocating a thumb. When my older son first showed me through his apartment, I was almost in shock. He was a Budweiser memorabilia collector. I'm sure that's not too uncommon for guys that age, but he had the **same** memorabilia on his bedroom walls that my younger son had on his. Both brothers also had the same Led Zeppelin poster; it was one of their favorite groups, and they had attended the same concert as it toured one season, in different states.*

Both of them play golf and have a real aptitude for math and electronics. The older one wound up becoming a CPA, but his hobby was tinkering with television repair. The younger one studied electronics servicing, did television repair, and now does business machines servicing. I have a daughter who is four years younger; she shares with her newly found brother their favorite fast food: a McDonald's hamburger with nothing on it! (65fp)

Confirmed by the studies of twins reared apart, the distinctives related in this chapter may be assumed in some way to be part of genetic makeup. These histories are beginning to answer the question of Why? Perhaps they tell us that many synchronicities are simply the result of a common genetic design.

13
Connected by Family Time

❖ *There is a time for everything, and a season for every activity under heaven: a time to be born and a time to die, a time to plant and a time to uproot, a time to kill and a time to heal, a time to tear down and a time to build, a time to weep and a time to laugh, a time to mourn and a time to dance, a time to scatter stones and a time to gather them, a time to embrace and a time to refrain, a time to search and a time to give up. . . . He has made everything beautiful in its time. He has also set eternity in the hearts of men; yet they cannot fathom what God has done from beginning to end.* (Ecclesiastes 3:1-6,11, NIV)

FAMILY TIME-TAGGED DNA

Australian psychoanalyst Averil Earnshaw (1987, 1990) has done research leading to her interesting hypothesis that *inherited* DNA reflects the emotional crises of one's parents: births, deaths, migration, major gains, and losses which occurred before one's birth. Similarly notable events after birth are *shared* events in *family time* that alter one's own DNA and reverberate as anniversary events in succeeding generations. They inexorably persist in "body memories," whether or not in conscious thought, and erupt in physical and emotional events at predictable ages. She has observed in a study of her clients and the biographies of historical figures that major life events, although they may be qualitatively different, occur at the same age for a child as for his same-sex parent. **"Family time is the bridge that offers understanding of the 'when' of events"** (1987, p. 220). Earnshaw cautioned against a claustrophobic feeling of predetermined lifetimes; while the timing of body changes and life events may indeed be preset by inner messages of DNA, free will and a conscious awareness are available to protect against hasty choices at critical ages.

In interviews to formally test her hypothesis, Earnshaw (1987) encountered unconscious resistance to the idea of time-linking with parents, but "once we accept the idea, and once we check it, the data are there, 'staring us in the face.' Literature is full of references to transmission in time 'even unto the third and fourth generations'" (p. 232). Earnshaw's postulates seem to agree with Kammerer's ideas mentioned in Chapter 7: the inheritance of acquired characteristics; and their expression in like-and-like seriality. They also begin to mesh with Buchheimer's statements (Chapter 10) of holographic memory as part of the body's genetic-experiential system. She explained:

> *It seems to me that repetitions of un-worked through experiences are transferred to the next generation. The modus operandi would be psychosomatic; that is, first the disturbance of genetic material by emotional and physical (internal) turbulence, and later the re-emergence of the age-linked traumatic event in the next generation.* (Earnshaw, 1987, p. 59)

Synchronicities in dates of family time were mentioned to me by 27 genetically related, reunited families. They included birth, death, marriage, and major life changes at meaningful dates or ages. Thirteen persons reported multiple incidents. Eight families told of matches in birthday dates. Nine reported coincidences in both family time and in the timing of search activity; for example, when her father died on her lost son's birthday, one mother was moved to search aggressively for him. This information may begin to answer **When?** Even in the absence of what Earnshaw referred to as shared experiences after birth, similar life-changing events sometimes erupt at age-determined times in adoption-separated families. A few examples are these:

> *My natural mother and I both married at 18 to truck drivers. We both had daughters at 19. We both had our second child at 21, and this child was not legitimate.* (30fc)

My daughter is an absolute genetic blueprint of me. I contacted her when she was 18 and learned that, like me, she got pregnant at 15. She miscarried, but had planned to surrender the child through people I had trained in the adoption agency I operate through my church. (26fp)

My birthmother had given me up when she was 21. When I was 21, I had an abortion. I felt it was strange, that both of us at the same point in our lives went through basically the same thing--the loss of a child. We both married at the age of 25 and gave birth at the age of 27; hers was her second birth, and mine was my first. Her wedding anniversary is December 28. The day I met my husband--the day we celebrate religiously as our traditional anniversary--is also December 28. I asked my mother, "I'm 33 years old; what do I have to look forward to?" She said, "Hopefully 27 years of a happy marriage." She has been married for 27 years, and I am very, very happily married and look forward to a long and prosperous marriage myself. (5fc)

An inexplicable network of time, numbers, and dates fits the Möbius band analogy--the touching of one person with other members of his human family, unknowingly, then surprisingly witnessed from a higher perspective after the missing information is provided. Birth, marriage, and death dates appear frequently. Family members are as fascinated with deciphering these interrelationships as have been past and contemporary thinkers. **In reunion, the *now* has a new awareness of the past, and a place from which to build the future.**

Fascinating to note are some birthday dates: The birth of my mother's last child was the same date as the birth of my first child--October 21. I thought that our first introduction to each other on the phone was significant, in that it occurred on her wedding anniversary. (7fc)

My son's second daughter was born exactly on my 45th birthday. I am also a second daughter, and I have two daughters myself, the second of whom I have great affinity with. (27fp)

I am all three in the adoption triangle and have been blessed to find my biological family, the daughter I gave up for adoption, but not yet my adopted son's biological family. The daughter I gave up for adoption shares the same birthday as one of my biological sisters. My adopted son's daughter shares the same birthday as another of my biological sisters. (1fpco)

I began my search prompted by a co-worker's pregnancy. After disclosing my long-held secret to her, she discovered an ad for ALMA (Adoptees Liberty Movement Association) in a journal in the obstetrician's office. I went to the library and discovered there were many organizations that supported search and reunion. This gave me the courage to begin my search. I knew where my daughter was in six weeks. I waited and prayed a year before contacting her. The coincidences began with the contact. My first phone call (an anonymous survey on higher education) was on June 23, the day a cousin who had been living with my husband and me moved out. I don't know what that has to do with it, but it is a fact. I might have been trying to replace one loss by regaining another.

    Then on August 2 I went through the ruse of conducting a survey on adoption; I asked her if she thought adult adoptees who are 18 or older should have the right to open their birth records. She said, "Yes, I think they do, because I am adopted, and I would like to find my birthmother." At that point I told her who I was; we talked for several hours. Her first marriage took place August 2. So our first real coincidence was that I called her on her anniversary. Her first marriage had dissolved in less than two years. The separation was painful, and I imagine her feelings around that date are intense. (14fp)

I searched for my mother through the agency in Montreal for over 10 years. We met two years ago, on the day before my 28th birthday. (70fc)

I can remember when I was in about the fifth grade, for at least two years in a row, I prepared for my adopted mom's birthday (mistakenly) for May 25, but her actual birthday is July 25. Now I know my birthmom's birthday is May 27! My girlfriend's mother's birthday is also May 27. (43mc)

BIRTH

Further meaningful circumstances surrounding birthdays and childbirth include these:

I was born on my mother's 40th birthday, so we both have the same birthday. (17fc)

Since finding my daughter, I discovered that her oldest child was born on my father's birthday, and her second child was born on my son's birthday. (37fp)

I gave birth to a daughter on my great-grandfather's birthday; my brother's first baby was born on my husband's birthday. (44fc)

My adoptive mother and my birthmother were born one day apart, and all three of us are under the star sign Pisces. I was born on my great-grandfather's birthday. (19fc)

My two girls were born in the same month as my mother's sons. She told me that when she was pregnant with me, she did not want me to be a girl. She always wanted a little girl, and when I was born she knew that she would never have another. She said she felt like God was punishing her for giving away the little girl he gave her. I'm doing my best to make that up to her now. (4fc)

DEATH

Incidents related to death sometimes involve anomalous knowing and timing. The story of a woman who repeatedly dreamed of her mother's illness and knew when she died is told in detail in Chapter 11. She experienced a similar tragedy in the premature death of an adoptive brother:

> *My adoptive brother was adopted from Italy when he was three, and he knew he had a blood brother. His whole life he wanted to know him. My brother was killed in a car accident when he was 21. Just a few days afterward, our adoptive family received a letter from Italy, from his brother, saying, "Oh, at last I have found you, my younger brother in America. I am so happy; I have been so alone my whole life." It was devastating. I immediately worried that this might happen to me and kept saying to the adoption agency, "I feel it will happen to me, if you don't help me!" They said, "That kind of thing doesn't happen twice." But it did; my mother died too. My adoptive brother and I had been very close; I learned Italian and went to Italy to meet his brother. (53fc)*

> *My son had an adoptive grandparent and a birth grandparent die on the same day. (35fp)*

> *My father, who died on my son's birthday, left me just enough money to conduct the search. (49fp)*

> *I got engaged on September 22, 1979--the same day my mother's father died. (4fc)*

> *My birthmother was made to relinquish me by her own mother. It was just after her mother's funeral that she got my first call, so it took her some time to integrate. (41fc)*

Some of the most heart-rending stories come from those who finally find their roots, only to discover a granite gravestone erected in front of the family tree:

My adoptive mother died recently of cancer. In going through her belongings, I found my adoption papers. I searched and found that my birthmother had died one week before of pancreatic cancer, at age 44. I've been having symptoms and am afraid I have it too. I will visit her grave and help relatives plant a flower. (39fc)

Although my mother and sister did the search work, I got to place the first telephone call to the family, after being reached by an intermediary. I sorrowfully learned it was the day of my brother's funeral, and they had just left the cemetery. My brother and I were born on the same day of the month, 27 months apart. I was conceived in the town where he was born; 2,000 miles from there, he was conceived in the area where I was raised and where I was tracked down through my adoptive parents. We both were ambidextrous, had been in the same kind of work, and had studied in Holland. The day of that first telephone conversation was also my adoptive father's birthday. (36fc)

I learned that my birthfather had passed away just nine months before I located his family. (52fc)

I am an adoptee who found some of my maternal family 10 years ago. My birthmother was deceased by the time I found them. One of the first things I asked was, "When did she die?" I could not wait to go home to see if I had written a recognition of it in my journal. The dates were indeed the same. I remember that day very well, and I wrote in my journal, "I feel someone close to me has died." (48fc)

My search took 25 years. Born in 1935, I found in 1985. My search finally, really took off in October of 1983. My birthmother died in September 1983. She donated her body to medical science, and her ashes were released after I found the family. I was my mother's pallbearer, carrying her ashes to her grave. Her only other child, my half brother, became a minister in 1983, and he gave the graveside service. We literally took shovels and buried her ourselves. (42fc)

SYNCHRONICITY AND REUNION

150

14
Significance of the Connection

> We should not pretend to understand the world only by the intellect; we apprehend it just as much by feeling. Therefore the judgment of the intellect is, at best, only a half-truth, and must, if it is honest, also admit its inadequacy. (Jung, 1971, p. 495)

A synchronicity is a coincidence that is meaningful to the participants--a unique, subjective experience. There seems to be a strong motivation for physical reunion between a mother and child; perhaps it comes from a biological longing for the lost part. A compulsion toward cognitive meaning-making may follow the numinous experience of reunion, to make some sort of sense out of the missing years, and to answer the lifelong questions, **Did I do the best thing? Was it God's will? Did my parents love me?** Perhaps by discovering and holding onto connections of synchronicity, families are enabled to bear the results of years of discontinuity.

Is remembering itself a victory against a system that told its clients to forget and to pretend? Is it a sanctification of the mother-child archetype? Is reunion a compelled, holy act? Afterward, when the frozen, black-and-white mental slides take on color and turn into movies, more and more memories come unbidden from a realm of their own. From their broken, interrupted world, survivors find pieces of ideas to weave into words. Thoughts too profound for ordinary prose often burst out in poetry, as though some truths are better expressed as enigmas.

SYNCHRONICITY AND REUNION

A poignant, one-woman stage drama has played to a circuit of adoption- and family-related audiences: *"...a name you never got"* [sic], created and performed by reunited birthmother Ronda Slater (1984). Sheila Ganz (1987), another reunited birthmother, who is producing a documentary film on adoption, also wrote and directed a drama: *pretend it didnt happen [sic]*. If I were to select music to accompany the convoluted emotions of union/loss/reunion, it might well be a sorrowful/rejoicing clarinet that pierces through the minor keys of Klezmer tunes.

For those who have discovered it, synchronicity takes the darkly awful puzzle of love, abandonment, and grief and sparks a hint of the awesome. Following are the types of meaning attributed by some of the persons who lived the stories told in the preceding chapters. Some caught glimpses of eternity through the windows of time. Many did not attempt an explanation beyond their feelings of awe. The more reflective comments fall generally into two major divisions: human relationships and metaphysical explanations.

HUMAN RELATIONSHIPS

Connection with birth family. The first statement is made by a woman who is not only an adoptee but a psychotherapist who works with all parties in the adoption triad and who trains others to do so:

> *Everyone has his own internal pace for search; it must be respected. There is fear of abandonment, rejection, loss of everything. After search, an adoptee belongs in neither place, and in both. These people have lost fantasies, lost histories. When you adopt a child, you adopt the entire birth family. Whether you like it or not, whether they are visible or not, they are really a part of that family. (41fc)*

> *I am very happy to have found my mother, my twin sister, two nephews, and a niece. Both my adoptive parents have passed away, and last year I lost an aunt with whom I was very close. I am very happily married, but sometimes you need a family too, you know. (67fc)*

Significance of the Connection

*My sister found our mother and me at a time in my life when I could handle it. Had she found me even a year earlier, it would not have been quite as easy for me to accept. She just picked the perfect time. It couldn't have been better. If someone would have planned this and said, "OK, this is a point in her life when she can handle all this," that would have been it. It was like we **meshed**. It amazes me. Now that we've become close, there is very definitely a feeling of oneness. When she gets depressed, I get depressed. If she's worried about something, I can feel it and call to talk to her; if I'm feeling really down, she'll give me a call. It's like we're on the same wave length. I believe people can be receptive to other people's feelings and thoughts, as long as they're willing to be receptive. (31fs)*

Both my birthparents had died previous to my finding the family. But I did find siblings, aunts, uncles, cousins, and one marvelous step-grandmother on my mother's side. They filled me in with wonderful profiles of my mother and father. Perhaps I would have more to share had I had the benefit of meeting my mother and father, but I feel fortunate at having what little I do have. (42fc)

I am an adoptee and have recently been rewarded with a happy ending after a two-year search. Not only did I find my birthmother but five brothers and sisters as well. It has been very exciting! A few things that I found out along the way are a bit weird or uncanny. (51fc)

Birthfather issues. The son whose mother had intuited his name (when a paper with his newborn footprints fluttered) was reached by an intermediary and has so far refused a relationship with her. She says:

All is not negative, though. I feel much better first of all just knowing that he survived birth, that he is happy and healthy. I know that he was married four years ago, and that he graduated from college last year. I also know that he grew up in the town where I live, and only moved away less than a month ago! I have pictures (from high school yearbooks at the library) and know that he looks so much like me that I almost wince when I look at his face in the pictures.

His birthfather has been very supportive every step of the way in the search, by mail and by telephone. He and I are planning to get together for the first time in 26 years to catch up on our lives and to exchange information about ourselves and our families (neither one of us is now married). We plan to compose a letter to be sent to our son, and to include pictures of all of us, to let him know he is thought of constantly, and that we all love him. Whenever he is ready (if ever) he can contact us. (45fp)

I think that my coincidences are important in that they show that a child can have much more in common with the father than the mother--something most birthmothers do not even want to think about. When I first saw my son as a little child, years before I made contact, my immediate impression was that he was just like his father, and would not want to know me--and that turned out to be exactly right. (11fp)

As it has turned out, I have taken on my family name, with my birthfather's permission. Our reunion was a very happy time for both of us, especially for me--to have my identity, and to be part of a family. It was uncanny as far as feeling like he has been in my life all my life. . . . Things were going along more than beautifully, until he told his wife, and we have not been able to have any contact since then. His wife was adopted; her mother was married five times, and I think she has had some great difficulty with that. . . . Unfortunately, the only people in his family that knew about me were his brother and his sister, and neither one of them has chosen to have any contact with me. A friend of mine wrote to this aunt, and both times the letters came back unopened. So it has been kind of tough for me, as far as that goes. (23fc)

Adoptive family issues

My adoptive mother died recently; my adoptive father does not know of my reunion, and I will not tell him. Both my adoptive parents were alcoholics. (39fc)

I have a poem written by my birthmother the night I was born. With each passing month I'm learning much, much more about myself and my birth family. [She contributed a long list of synchronicities and genetic *similarities to this study.] However, I am the product of heredity and environment (my adoptive family), just as every adoptee is. Just how much is genetic and how much is a result of my environmental influences, I am not sure. According to my (full, blood) sister, I am one of the most balanced people that she has met. I have my adoptive parents to thank for this characteristic. In fact, if I had hand-picked them myself, I couldn't have chosen better. They are the most wonderful people in my life. (19fc)*

Coincidences or serendipitous encounters between members of the extended adoptive and birth families through the years are often mentioned. Some of them may be related to the former practice of selective placement, the matching of birth and adoptive families according to national origin, talents, and other characteristics. Other aspects are in the realm of the unexplainable.

My daughter's adoptive mother and I share the same first name, the same age, ethnic background, coloring, and mannerisms. She kept the same name for our daughter that I had given her. We have all been struck by these and other similarities in educational background, family size, etc. (6fp)

I know very little about my surrendered son. Since I found him he has wanted very little to do with me. From what I have seen, he is not much like me, but a lot like his birthfather and like my present husband, to whom he is not related. The most amazing thing in my case is that my son and my husband work in the same field of computer science--so close that my husband's company bought a program from my son's company, and they are on the same computer bulletin board. My husband says this is most unlikely, given the present vastness of the computer field. My husband has identified himself to my son, and they have had some communication over the past year. Apparently he is more like my husband in aptitudes and interests than our kids at home, even though he is not a blood relative. This is ironic and one more thing to make me sad; had I kept him, he would have had a step-dad that he could relate to. In fact, my husband is a lot like the natural father; they are both super-bright, scientific types who like classical music. (11fp)

During our first visit to my mother's home, my husband said while we were getting ready for bed, "I don't know if I should say this." I said, "What? Go ahead." He went on, "I just can't get over how much your birthmother is like the mother who raised you: their temperament, the things they like to do, their hobbies, gardening, and crafts." Also, her new husband is so much the same temperament as the dad who raised me; they like a lot of the same things. My mother had me when she was only 13 years old. She found me because she had remarried, told her story to her new husband, and he promised he would help find her children. (18fc)

My adoptive and birth parents are all from the South. Although from different states, they have the same drawl and the same mannerisms. The last names of my birthfather, birthmother, and adoptive family all begin with the same letter. (5fc)

In 1961, when our missing child's adoptive family purchased a business with a distinctive Indian logo, I bought an outfit for our younger daughter with the same large emblem on it; we have a picture to confirm the fact. (36fp)

At one time, when working as a waitress, I served my son's adoptive mother. I have learned that she and I work just three doors apart. (21fp)

My adoptive father and my birthfather both worked on the same wharf for 35 years in different jobs. (19fc)

One of the strangest coincidences is that both of my fathers--natural and adoptive--are electricians; and both of their fathers are also electricians. Another strange thing is that my adoptive sister is left-handed, while both of her natural parents (my adoptive parents) are right-handed; whereas I am right-handed, and my natural parents are both left-handed. So we're mirror images of each other. She's their natural child, but obviously has been my sister all my life. (23fc)

I spent an enjoyable week visiting my daughter's [...] 22 years older than me. We wept together that [...] we could meet. We marveled that all four of us [...] birth) had been born in the same state, and yet the [...] another, distant state. He and I laughed to disco[...] experience in common. As youngsters in schools separated by 50 miles and one generation, we had each been asked by our orchestra directors to "fill in" on the bassoon for a special music contest performance--but just to sit there, look competent, and pretend to play! (36fp)

My husband's half brother was a performer in a nightclub for a time and was in a show that his adoptive parents attended while visiting Reno. No one ever suspected their paths were crossing. (55fo)

Medical history is taken for granted and easily obtained in ordinary families, but adoptees usually must undergo treatment with minimal, zero, false, or never-updated information about their families of origin:

Especially when a person is married and getting to the childbearing age, you need to know your medical history. Yet the way the adoption laws are, you never fully become an adult as an adopted person. Legally, in whatever state you live, you can inherit, vote, gamble, drink, and drive. But as an adoptee you never acquire an age when you are an adult. For example, even at age 46, if I go into an adoption office and say that I am looking for my birthmother or my birth sister, they say, "We need your mother's signature before anything can happen." This is ridiculous. (53fc)

I am in recovery from alcoholism and drug addiction, and they say that working through these issues is important to recovery. I tend to avoid (close to deny) a lot of my adoption issues and have only recently begun to re-examine them. My birthmother tried to keep me for nine months, but succumbed and signed the papers in 1942. One of the reasons for my search centered on my alcoholism, and I wanted to know family medical history to see if it was in my ancestry. (43mc)

Personal development involves filling in the missing pieces:

I am a psychotherapist myself and have worked through large amounts of the pain of this loss in my life. I feel like I am on the verge of something good as this story unfolds. (46fp)

It makes me feel so much sadder for my child, to learn now about prenatal memory. (10fp)

Over the years I have blocked many things from my mind about our separation. I was successful in this; if I had not moved on, I may not have survived such a tragic and heartbreaking ordeal. And for 13 years we were living within 50 miles of each other! (15fp)

[From the woman who found the connection with her grandfather and the Red Cross, showing how important finding "information" is]: At the Red Cross office I asked if they might have an address on his daughter (my birthmother). The lady said to me, "Well, let me go look in the file, and I will make a copy of whatever is in there and send it to you." **My whole life had been "look in the file and let me see what is there"** *(but kept secret). This woman, I know, didn't realize what she did for me, and how strong and empowered I felt by that comment! She was a very nice person, and has continued to be helpful to me. It was also the first person I have ever talked to who actually* **knew** *any of my birth family. As she told me about my grandfather, I thought to myself, "He seems like he was a nice guy." That's important, too. (2fc)*

Beginning in 1953, I made a special effort to find and talk with other adopted people. I learned from them that they shared many of my characteristics and problems. Motivated now by more than a desire to find my mother, wanting now to satisfy her desire to know me (I now assumed she had this desire), but also strengthened by the discovery of the hidden world of adoption-in-adulthood, I finally did what I could have done many years before. I found her. . . . I went into the room where my mother was, she again in tears, and we embraced. Then we sat down on the sofa and began to talk together and look at each other.

    She wanted to tell me of my birth, my early infancy, and most of all how she had wanted to keep me. I told her where I had lived and how I had gone about finding her. Still crying but sometimes now laughing, my mother reigned supreme on this day of her glory. For the love she had never forsaken lived again in this stranger who had come into her home. She died at the age of 80 in 1967. Her inner life was seldom revealed. But once she wrote to one of my friends: "I lay at night thinking of my wonderful daughter and how thankful I am to have her back again; and thinking of her dad, too. When you see (him) never mention that to him. I think my love is stronger for her than if I could have kept her. Oh dear! It is a good thing no one can read our minds. Someone said one time, 'Only God can.' I said, 'Yes.'" (40fc)

Acceptance of what's left is a positive way of reframing the loss of the years that have gone before:

My heart is full of love for my son, and to find that he turned out to be such a good person is very humbling indeed. We can't turn back the clock, and neither would we wish to. I can't take him back, and he has had a loving and close-knit family around him. All I ask is for some room around the sides of his life, and pray that we can all enrich each other's lives as the future unfolds. (27fp)

My mother is 80 years old now and in a nursing home, and I visit her often. (24fc)

METAPHYSICAL EXPLANATIONS
God's involvement

As a child I always felt special, as though someone from above was taking care of me, as well as my wonderful parents here on earth. It seemed only natural that when I found my birthmother, she would also be a kind, loving Christian. I was also a new Christian at the time of our meeting. I feel that our "miracle meeting" was truly blessed by God. I remember after three years of searching, I finally prayed for help in finding her. My prayers were answered in my husband, who mentioned that I might write letters to certain people; sure enough, that very simple idea led to our initial contact. Once I had prayed about this, I had no doubts at all--I would not be turned away by my mother, but would be accepted somehow. I still consider our meeting a miracle, and it has only strengthened my faith in God's power. I do feel much more at ease--for myself and my children. Now that I know where I come from, they also know where their roots lie. (7fc)

I was amazed. My mother reached me when I was 44. In my teen years I probably had some fantasies that one day my birthparents would find me. I learned that I was born when my mother was 13; she said that during holidays and my birthday she would think about me and wonder if I had a good home and if I was OK. At our reunion, she kept saying, "I'm so thankful that I found you and that you had a good home." It seemed like God worked out the search; it was so easy for her. The fact that my adoptive parents had such an unusual name made it easy. I think she has peace and contentment to know where we are. I was surprised, but not shocked, because I really feel that the Lord had prepared me for the reunion. It's like we've been doing things together all along. (18fc)

I found my daughter when she was 14 but waited to age 18 to contact her. I believe I was led of the Lord and waited for his timing. Separation by adoption affected my life. I changed my career choice because of it--from nursing to social welfare. I have done research on how all Bible adoption was "open" and promote pro-life, open adoption. (26fp)

My birthmother's husband told me that every year on my birthday, the first thing when he woke up, he would pray that one day I'd come to find her, because that was the only day of the year that she really allowed herself to think about me, to grieve, and she was always very upset. He knew about me before they were married, when I was 10 months old. (44fc)

I made a promise and fulfilled an obligation. I told the caseworker that handled the adoption that someday I would find my son. I said, "When he turns 18 years old, I am going to start looking, and I am not going to stop until I find him." Before we married, I told my husband the circumstances, the fact that I had a son out there, and that I would be looking for him at a certain point. I feel that God led me in the right way, because there were so many things that could have prevented me from ever finding him. The fact that I tuned in the right TV program, got hold of a person who could help, then stopped to ask directions of a person 350 miles away who knew my son and gave me information, seems to prove it was meant to be. (65fp)

I believe God decided this was the time for it to happen, since everything fell into place in less than a week, after four years of trying. It was just such a coincidence. It has all been such an amazing and rewarding experience since the search has been completed. (55fo)

My explanation for all of these coincidences is that finding out I was adopted, finding my birthmother, and continuing a relationship with her, my half brothers and half sister was "meant to be." I think God knew I had that need to feel complete and happy. (63mc)

Wonder

What is the probability that in a city of a million people the son of a birthfather would unknowingly go to live in a rehabilitation home with three other children, one of whom was a daughter of the adopting family (whose other daughter was his, for whom he had been searching)? Interesting, don't you think? (8mp)

*I'm interested in synchronicity. I'm reading a book called **The Road Less Traveled**, the chapter on grace and synchronicity, where Peck talks about all these phenomena: the things that happen, that don't seem to have an explanation. But it's like there **is** something there, every time my daughter brings up something, like that fact that we both were in a bike accident and broke a front tooth in the same year. (32fp)*

I have no idea how to explain our coincidences. I don't know that it would be telepathy, but there's bound to be some reason. It means there's a lot of congruity in the world. I can put in a spiritual factor, perhaps. Or there may be some kind of genetic concept that goes down through the ages. (56mc)

Destiny

Every time we speak or get together, we find another common denominator, and it's not just something like we both like fried chicken! There are definite things. It's almost like my mother lived her life and created a path, and then I lived it. We married similar men. I followed the same order of life events. I have no evidence as to what would cause something like this, but I think that people have a destiny. You can change it, and you can divert from it, but basically your whole plan of life is pretty well ironed out the minute you are born. You can deviate from it, but if you stay on what you feel might be the right way to go with your life, it is already preplanned. Whether or not that comes from your genes--it could very well be. It's weird: Here are a mother and daughter who have been separated since birth--31 years; we get together and realize that our paths have been almost identical! (5fc)

Spirit of deceased relative. The feelings expressed by the mother in the following reflection are like those of Alex Haley in *Roots* (1976), who walked into his ancestral village in West Africa at the very hour his 83-year-old Cousin Georgia died in a Kansas City hospital: "I think that as the last of the old ladies who talked the story on Grandma's front porch, it had been her job to get me to Africa, then she went to join the others up there watchin'" (p. 581).

Significance of the Connection

How do I explain these things? I think they're spiritual. I believe in spirits, which may be of people who are no longer alive, who have been alive at one time. They're trying to help you make connections, maybe. My father died on my son's birthday. In a way, when something like that happens, you feel the person who died is happy in your meeting another part of your own family whom you've never met before. You have a loss, but you are also finding someone at the same time. When I first met my son, I felt like a weight was lifted off my shoulders. I literally, physically felt that. I feel that he and I share a lot in common, and we have the potential for being very close. (49fp)

My brother learned my name six weeks before he died. He passed away three days before I placed my first call to the family, on the day of his funeral. My mother thinks he had a part in interceding with God for an end to her long search. (36fc)

Extrasensory perception

*[From the adoptee who shared her mother's love of Elvis Presley, had used her mother's name in childhood play, and whose mother was also living in Arizona at the time of finding]: I have been reluctant to draw many conclusions about these events, but I always **knew** that I would find my mother. She and I have often spoken at length about some of these strange things. She is a deeply religious woman and believes that God is/was responsible. I am more inclined toward thinking that she and I did communicate over the years. It's the Arizona connection that gets me--of all the God-forsaken places! It is difficult in this age to learn to trust one's instincts; we aren't too well connected with listening to our inner voices. I'm truly blessed that I listened and was able to respond. (12fc)*

   [Continuing now in her other role of birthmother still in search of a son]: I'm trying to do this as I search for my son. He is in need of me; I know this. It is traumatic for my other children and my husband to have me so focused on this. It's like waking in the night for no reason, and then hearing my three-year-old son fall out of bed five minutes later because he had a bad dream about monsters. I am terrified that my (older, lost) son is in real, deep trouble; I hope this is not later proved true. (12fp)

I explain it [thinking of son at critical times] as "vibes" or psychic energy. (35fp)

I believe in ESP, and that a genetic connection increases the ability for it. (36fc)

There are numerous incidents in my life, all unexplainable in the natural. I want to study these things and research how they happen. I need to learn how to read the messages I receive. I am about to start studies at college in psychology, as the mind and how it works has me fascinated. I need to understand what has happened to me all my life--and still is--because at times the feelings are so strong, and I don't know what I am meant to do. It is very frustrating, to say the least. I cannot explain my visions, just to say I have them. I see things, places, people--and later on I meet them or find out they connect me with my real family. (30fc)

One part of the mind can play some truly strange games with other parts, something we've known for a long time. But how can phenomena like this be explained away as suppression or desires of the unconscious? To bring in another element, by way of explanation, I have a fair amount of faith in the so-called pseudo-science of parapsychology. I studied it in college--right along with "normal" psychology--and am convinced that we all possess varying degrees and types of psychic abilities. After all, we only use about one eighth of our brainpower, or so scientists tell us. So what happens to the other seven eighths?
    *Many things are possible of the human mind, so clairvoyance is certainly a possibility, just as is psychokinesis, telepathy, precognition, and so forth. To varying degrees, it explains the wanderlust. It's all part of "The Search," even if we don't recognize it as such at the time. I hitchhiked around the entire country from the time I was about 15--looking for something. I didn't know then what it was, but in retrospect I can see it. Some psychologists might explain this behavior as running--running **away** from this and that. But I wonder if they've considered that it might be running **to** something--family--even if we didn't know exactly what it was we were chasing at the time? Like the proverbial cat who instinctively knows how to return home from almost anywhere, maybe some humans, too, have an innate ability--and a need--to find their blood bonds.* (22mc)

MEANING AND SIGNIFICANCE

Subjective words, visual images, and feelings are the essence of synchronicity, rather than accumulated, objective data. Numinous experience and cognitive meaning-making are like a synesthesia, alternating as stimuli and joining in response. Many of the family members did not attempt a verbal expression of their feelings, beyond surprise and wonder, at the discovery of coincidences and the overall synchronicity of reunion.

Twenty-two persons expressed the meaning of their experiences in terms of personal development and human relationships, using such phrases as:

connection, we meshed, a feeling of oneness, in common, my identity, a complete person, part of a family, my ancestry, love, and *a happy ending*.

Nineteen persons described a more metaphysical meaning-making in numinous language. Eight felt God's direct, personal involvement, mentioning:

prayer, timing, meant to be, prepared me, led me, planned, and *our miracle meeting*.

Eleven others described a sense of higher purpose, destiny, or extrasensory connection at work, in such terms as:

there is something there, congruity in the world, preplanned, a destiny, identical paths, trust one's instincts, our inner voices, psychic energy, ESP, telepathy, precognition, clairvoyance, unexplainable in the natural, and *an innate ability and need to find blood bonds*.

ADDITIONAL OBSERVATIONS

An egocentric bias in assigning subjective meaning may pervade the anecdotes of synchronicity, and with an unusual strength and power, because the other person who was lost and has been found is thought of as part of one's own "self." Infants were taken from their mothers while still in primal relationship with them. At the time of surrender, many birthmothers were young teenagers, not yet fully individuated themselves. **A searching person may feel a need to find the missing part, and after reunion may continue to sort for "sameness," to be convinced that the parts match and that the puzzle is**

solved. The participants seem to confirm the reports of other studies, that there is no centeredness for one's ego until completion of the circle, until missing information is supplied.

It may be hypothesized that identity and selfhood are actualized through reunion. Jung saw the individuation process as the lens through which he viewed all religious experience, even regarding the individuation process as a spiritual journey in itself (Aziz, 1990). After the self-actualizing peak experience (Maslow, 1964) of reunion, it was described by many in spiritual terms. An applicable statement may be that of Grof (1985). He summarized the data of Maslow, Jung, and others, as well as his own deep experiential work:

> *According to the new data, spirituality is an intrinsic property of the psyche that emerges quite spontaneously when the process of self-exploration reaches sufficient depth. Direct experiential confrontation with the perinatal and transpersonal levels of the unconscious is always associated with a spontaneous awakening of a spirituality that is quite independent of the individual's childhood experiences, religious programming, church affiliation, and even cultural and racial background. The individual who connects with these levels of his or her psyche automatically develops a new world view within which spirituality represents a natural, essential, and absolutely vital element of existence.* (p. 368)

Several participants in this study expressed surprise at their own new sense of spirituality, prefacing comments about God's timing or action in the reunion with, "I'm not a religious person, but . . ." In his book on the inextricable relationship of spiritual and psychological human functioning, psychologist David G. Benner (1988) wrote, "False selves can only be *defended*; only true selves can be *transcended*" (p. 123). **For parents and children whose lives before reunion were based on elements of falsehood and denial, a true and complete selfhood after reunion seems to activate movement in the direction of freedom and transcendence.**

15
Synchronicity's Implications

Family separation through the social and legal practice of closed, secret adoption has been generally viewed as pervasively stressful. Chronicles ensuing from the recent phenomenon of reunion have catalyzed specific attention on the psychological trauma of loss, the therapeutic value of search, and the transpersonal aspects of a genetic family system or clan.

Singly and as a collection, the anecdotes of synchronicity add a new dimension to the sociological and historical dilemma. We must consider what they reveal about a society that separated families and then explicitly or implicitly said to each person: You must get on with your life and pretend your other family members do not exist and are not longing for you; you must never ask questions about their names, location, activities, or welfare; there is no need for you to know such things as dates of marriage, childbirth, death, and onset of specific medical problems; you will survive without opportunity to express love, to marvel at your genetic idiosyncrasies, and to confirm your history and your selfhood.

The anecdotes in this collection leave a suggestion about the effects of a lack of such information. Even in the most dysfunctional or feuding of families, such minimal data is ordinarily tracked in a kind of oral history. **The adoption-separated genetic family system may have such a need for information (either consciously or unconsciously) that the transcendent Creator, or the laws of the universe, or the human mind makes a supernatural or anomalistic psychological attempt to fill it.** Does morphic resonance or the law of seriality have a goal-oriented function behind the scenes in this drama, pulling like and like together?

The message to those families still searching for one another may be to listen to their intuition and to know that their lives are an interwoven system.

Like the Möbius-connection paradigm, joined but experienced from limited dimensions, they may imagine this system like a hologram, one day to be viewed from a higher dimension of reunion, with all the missing information supplied.

The pattern may be far more than the line-by-line completion of a genealogical chart. What are the sparkling filaments and knots of coincidence that link a broken Gestalt and fit neither words nor ordinary notions? The stories of synchronicity have looked at the past and the present, and they have something to say about the future. They may speak in a small voice, but with reverberating overtones. Reunions like these are not a minor footnote to history; they promise major volumes to come.

DISCUSSION OF THE COLLECTED UNION/LOSS/REUNION HISTORIES

All of the anecdotes are evidence of a connection. Some may be pure chance; all are coincidence. More than that, they have **meaning** for the storytellers, and therefore are raised to the level of synchronicity. **Reunion itself is a synchronicity.** Anecdotes of subjective events included some forms of waking impressions, hallucinations, and vivid dreams, sufficiently marked out in the mind so that when correlation with objective occurrences was later confirmed, there was no doubt as to the certainty that the coincidences were meaningful. The writers communicated their discoveries and their interpretations, integrating their own identities in the process.

The fact that anecdotes were told by 68 women and eight men may indicate that women are more likely to talk about the emotional connectedness that is essential to their development (Miller-Havens, 1990), but not that men do not have synchronicities or intuitive experiences; 67 paragraphs described coincidences involving men. Most of the contributors were residents of the United States (from 24 states), with a few from Canada, England, New Zealand, and Western Australia. Anomalous experiences occurred and were consciously remembered at ages from preschool through adulthood. Unconscious material from prenatal and infancy periods was also conceptualized and understood by adoptees after reunion, either in therapy or in conversation with birthparents.

For reconnected families, synchronicity seems to give a sense of focus to a backward look at a hazy past. Interpretations do not belong to the outsider, nor are they necessarily subject to Jungian analysis. With some aberrations, of course, there is a lifelong bond between a mother and her child. For those who have endured the trauma of separation by adoption and the struggle of search, in the absence of a lifetime of other evidence, the discovery and integration of synchronicities serve to confirm, support, and deepen their bond.

A mother, particularly, seems to cling to what she *does* know--love--as she searches for meaning. For the typical mother in this study, who missed seeing her child's first steps, science projects, and high school graduation, that meaning is simply that her constant love was endorsed in the interim by small but awesome proofs that now serve to strengthen the cord of an enduring connection.

For the person who encounters rejection or death at the end of a search, synchronicities take on additional importance; if there is to be no continuing relationship, the meaningful coincidences may be all one has. For the reunited child, parents, and siblings, a critical significance in the synchronicities may be in what they validate for the individual: **There is someone else in the world designed a lot like me who was aware of my existence; I am OK after all.**

IMPLICATIONS FOR FUTURE RESEARCH

My descriptive, observational study has generated a significant amount of information about the dynamics of (a) genuinely moving coincidences and (b) the genetic family system. The anecdotes in their present form are open to continued exploratory analysis for pattern and structure. In addition, suggestions for further research include:

1. **Genograms** (Bowen, 1978; Marlin, 1989; McGoldrick & Gerson, 1985) could be used in a detailed, post-reunion study of synchronicity in major life events, as well as in physical, personality, and spiritual characteristics. Questions related to what occurred in the grandparents' lives when they were the same age as the surrendering birthparents would further the research into Earnshaw's (1987, 1990) hypothesis of age-linked family time.

2. Tracking the **lifetime travel patterns** of separated family members would add dimension to a study of homing mechanisms as possibly related to

DNA, memory, or the earth's electromagnetic fields. The influence of genetic or prenatal memory is ideally studied in persons who have lived apart from their biological families. Imaginative research could evolve from these concepts.

3. While twins provide a greater quantity of like genes for comparison, the **genetic mix** of any adoptee, siblings, and parents is a resource for a variety of hypotheses for apparent coincidences in such factors as religion, language, and cultural styles. Current longitudinal studies, such as those of the Colorado Adoption Project and the Minnesota Center for Twin and Adoption Research, will contribute answers and raise additional questions concerning normative development during separation.

4. Research into **states of consciousness** when having premonitions of crisis or when selecting vacation locations, occupations, hobbies, or names would be intriguing. A study of how neurological functioning differs between occasions of intuition and the ordinary cognitive states of reasoning and analysis might follow. What is the difference between deliberately trying to think of a lost child's unknown name versus having it come spontaneously? An experiment could be performed with parents and children still in search, asking them to record names they might expect to find, and the manner in which the names were determined; after reunion, the results could be analyzed. It might be assumed that an adoptee's knowing a mother's name comes from unconscious memory storage, whereas a mother's knowing a name selected for the child by adoptive parents would have a more anomalous transfer or creation of information. What determines the sensory modalities through which anomalous information arises? Participants in the current study had: (a) visual representations in dreams or art (53fc, 57fp, 70fc); (b) internal auditory reception of a name (36fp, 45fp); and (c) kinesthetic sensations when nearing critical locations (30fc, 48fc).

5. Qualitative studies of **psychological and personality factors** could answer such questions as: (a) Are psychological factors a major cause of perceived coincidence?; (b) What personality factors may differentiate those persons who do and do not report experiences of synchronicity? (In this study, 66 of the primary respondents were the searchers, and four of them were those persons who were first located by the others, or "found." What does this

imply?); and (c) Might the rate of noticing synchronicities change with training or trust of such experiences?

6. Further investigation specifically coordinated with the challenge of a **critical incidence study** (Diaconis and Mosteller, 1989) could add to the scientific base of meaningful coincidences between separated family members. The phenomenological-descriptive nature of this research is fundamental, but further systematic studies could be done, with attention to clear demarcation between observed experiences and extrapolation, or between the events of coincidence and the psychological factors involved in meaning-making.

7. A **comparison study** might be made among families of closed, secret adoption versus families involved in open adoption arrangements, to explore similarities or differences in the categories and frequency of meaningful coincidences reported.

8. Adoption as a social institution is changing, with a trend toward truth and openness (Arms, 1990; Baran & Pannor, 1990a, 1990b; Brodzinsky & Schechter, 1990; Chapman, Dorner, Silber, & Winterberg, 1986, 1987; Griffith, 1991; Kirk, 1985; McRoy, Grotevant, & White, 1988; Sorosky et al., 1978). The complexity of adoption is no longer of concern only to social service professionals. It has recently attracted interdisciplinary interest; questions have already been raised in areas of behavioral genetics, prenatal and humanistic psychology, attachment theory, psychiatry, clinical medicine and nursing, law, and special education. The material in this study confirms a pressing need for **systematic research** of a phenomenological-descriptive variety in these and other related disciplines.

9. There is a lack of material on adoption's life-course impact in most psychology and human development textbooks. Even the word *adoption* is missing from countless indices, a result of the past practice of pretending that a family affected by adoption is just like any other. The reunion histories of the past two decades, including those in this book, demand the **rewriting of texts**, to include the latest research and to stimulate more.

IMPLICATIONS FOR COUNSELING PSYCHOLOGY

These stories have exhibited the fact that in many ways the status of a birth family system does not end at surrender, and that birth and adoptive families have an intergenerational connection. Adoption is not a one-time event, a solution, or a concept. Once tilted into motion, it is a lifelong balancing process lived by emotional, spiritual, flesh-and-blood individuals. The narratives in this collection imply that Western society has erred: (a) in being too quick to impose a higher value on a healthy single mother's education, career, and momentary pride, than on nature's intent for breast-feeding and keeping genetically related families together; and (b) in employing closed, secret policies when families must be separated, eliminating the flow of necessary information between their members.

There will always be children who truly need homes, and for many of them adoption or guardianship will continue to be a positive way of providing those homes. But, as A. B. Brodzinsky (1990) pointed out, it has been common knowledge among professionals that, with a few recent attempts to the contrary (Child Welfare League of America, 1988; Moore & Burt, 1982; O'Leary, Shore, & Wilder, 1984), a greater commitment of services and resources has been made to support the relationship between a child and the adoptive parents than between that same child and the birthparents (Bernstein, 1963; Child Welfare League of America, 1960; Kadushin, 1974; Riben, 1988; Sorich & Siebert, 1982).

For many separated persons, an unspoken, deep need for reunion pervades their lives. There is an urgent demand for clinical services to catch up to this reality. Integration of professional and self-help support resources, through training and restructuring, is called for. The value of reunited persons as professional or lay wounded healers is inestimable, as they acknowledge the roles of self-examination, hard work, and intuition in a successful search. Additional research for the writing of helping manuals could spring from the work done by D. M. Brodzinsky and Schechter (1990); Griffith (1991); Rando (1986); Rillera (1987, 1991); Silverman (1981); Sorosky et al. (1978); and Winkler et al. (1988).

Post-reunion work with adoptive and birth families is a new field for family systems therapists, and more must be trained in methods of successful integration. Post-reunion relationships range from delightful to distressing. As at any age, an adopted person's adjustment is partially determined by the adoptive parents' acceptance of the reality of two sets of parents (Adelberg, 1986; D. M. Brodzinsky, 1987; D. M. Brodzinsky et al., 1986). Adequately prepared inter- and intrapersonal therapists are able to help consolidate or prevent troublesome post-reunion relationships in newly acquainted adoptive and birth families, as well as in families of open adoption. The establishment of such therapy and consulting services is beginning to spread across the United States, following the lead of veteran social workers like Annette Baran, Reuben Pannor, and Sharon Kaplan in California (for list, see Lifton, 1988; or contact support groups in Appendix).

Adoptee Joyce Pavao (1989), a social worker with a doctorate in education from Harvard, operates an innovative clinic applying family systems therapy to the extended families of adoption. It includes a program to train other professionals, called the Pre- and Post-Adoption Consulting Team (PACT), at the Family Center and Adoption Resource Center in West Somerville, Massachusetts. Teaching that there are normative crises in the developmental stages of all members of the adoption triad, she takes a systemic approach based on the theories of Erik Erikson, David Kantor, and Robert Kegan. Said Pavao (1989):

> *Adoption is an ever-evolving process. We used to think the court procedure was the end. Then we thought reunion was the end. Now we are finding it never ends; there are more issues post-search than ever before.*

It is important that helping professionals expand their ideas of post-adoption services and examine their own values and beliefs about search and reunion; either positive pressure or negative disapproval may interfere with the intention of treatment. **Uniquely specialized therapy is appropriate for each person in the extended families of birth and adoption. The integration of synchronicities and their significance could be a vital part of that therapy.**

Summary: Connection Through Information

The reunion of adoptees with their birth families and the subsequent discovery of awe-inspiring, humorous, or simply surprising incidents of synchronicity have been reported and categorized from observation points ranging from philosophy to genetics. Anecdotes have confirmed in a unique way the relevance of **information**: (a) the trauma of the lack of it for separated family members; (b) the therapeutic value of its acquisition through search and reunion; (c) its meaning and unifying power in the form of synchronicity; (d) its numinous source in universal truths; (e) its expression in numbers, names, and verbal concepts; (f) its storage in various types of memory; (g) its anomalous transfer in flashes of intuition or telepathy; and (h) its timed, regulated transfer through genetic mechanisms.

The kinds of information regarded by 70 reunited families as highly meaningful correspondence of space, time, and circumstance during the years of their separation fell into these general categories:

- 55.7% reported intersection in **place or location** (residence, migration, vacation, and search).

- 50.0% found meaning in **genetic architecture** (idiosyncrasies, occupation, religiosity, education, grooming, mating, collecting, handwriting, voice, etc.).

- 45.7% had one or multiple matches in significant **names**.

- 38.6% had synchronicity in dates of major life events in **family time**.

- 32.9% discovered synchronicity in **timing of search activity**.

- 32.9% experienced accurate **dreams or intuition** (7 as young children; 20 as adults).

- 24.3% had anomalous experiences with a possible **memory** component (genetic, prenatal, or preseparation).

It is not reasonable to generalize from these data, because relationships are still developing, and the initial anecdotes are not the totality of synchronicities being uncovered. The reports were self-selected and open-ended, and a detailed questionnaire was not used.

The histories of the 70 families seem to support the findings of developmental behavioral geneticists that DNA, which is present in all body cells as the repository of inherited characteristics, carries programs which fire at various times, affecting physical growth and decline, personality, choices, and major life events. There is speculation that the RNA which may carry memory has prenatal, genetic, and cellular input. Further, it is thought that the psychological depth of the engram, the permanent effect of memory, when a mother and child are unnaturally separated, contributes to a wrenching, primal injury.

I believe this study has suggested interrelationships between psychopathology (separation and loss), psychophysiology (longing and pain), and the anomalistic psychological phenomena of intuition, telepathy, and synchronicity. These phenomena seem to be related to a human being's deepest yearnings, repressions, doubts, and faith. Separation by closed, secret adoption has lifelong effects, characterized by feelings of abandonment in the children and grief in the parents. **A cathexis or emotional investment in the separated persons may serve to predispose and strengthen the likelihood of synchronicity in their lives.**

This book is not presumed to be a definitive psychology with a set of unifying interpretations; nor is it merely a fanciful exercise of the imagination. It is rather a series of descriptive slices from the layers of history of a scattered sample of parents and their adult children who are forging their own experiments and making their own conclusions. The data will continue to be assembled, in order to comprehend a surprising but common-sense connection that endures through union, loss, and reunion.

By now it seems to me, an inquisitive observer/participant, that a living family system, unnaturally broken, continues to be governed by mechanistic DNA, but with a purposeful movement that enfolds information or memory and unfolds a transcendent awareness of the missing parts; and that there is a natural balance of causal and acausal factors in that movement. The psychic nexus of consciousness and the concept of teleology in space-time raise the idea of tapping into a universal wisdom, that place of archetypes, algorithms, and names inscribed in the Book of Life.

Kammerer gave clues to a principle that pulls like and like together in a pattern; Sheldrake saw form and pattern in a system where information from all past members influences the present; Jung described common designs in the network of a patternweaver. Reunited families often express an awareness of a master plan that leaves them with the same sense described by William James (1920):

> In the pulse of inner life immediately present now in each one of us is a little past, a little future, a little awareness of our own body, of each other's persons, of these sublimities we are trying to talk about, of the earth's geography and the direction of history, of truth and error, of good and bad, and of who knows how much more? (pp. 286-287)

THE END/THE BEGINNING

APPENDIX

ADOPTION SUPPORT AND REUNION RESOURCES
(PROVIDING REFERRALS TO LOCAL GROUPS AND THERAPISTS)

Adoptees Liberty Movement Association (ALMA)
P.O. Box 154, Washington Bridge Station
New York City, NY 10033

Adoption and Family Reunion Center
P.O. Box 1860
Cape Coral, FL 33910

Adoption Counselling Centre and Birthlink Register
12 Castle Street, Second Floor
Edinburgh, Scotland EH2 3DN

Adoptive Parents for Open Records (APFOR)
P.O. Box 193
Long Valley, NJ 07853

American Adoption Congress (AAC)
1000 Connecticut Avenue NW, Suite 9
Washington, DC 20036

Concerned United Birthparents (CUB)
2000 Walker Street
Des Moines, IA 50317

Council for Equal Rights in Adoption (CERA)
401 East 74th Street
New York City, NY 10021

Department of Social Welfare (Adoptions)
Private Bag, Postal Center
Wellington, New Zealand

International Soundex Reunion Registry (ISRR)
P.O. Box 2312
Carson City, NV 89702

Adoption Support and Reunion Resources

Jigsaw
GPO 5260 BB, Melbourne 30001
Victoria, Australia

National Organization for Birthfathers and Adoption Reform
P.O. Box 1993 (NOBAR)
Baltimore, MD 21203

National Organization for the Counselling
of Adoptees and Parents (NORCAP)
3 New High Street
Headington, Oxford
England OX3 7AJ

Orphan Voyage
2141 Road 2300
Cedaredge, CO 81413

Parent Finders National Capital Region
P.O. Box 5211, Station F
Ottawa, Ontario
Canada K2C 3H5

Parent Finders of Canada
1408 West 45th Avenue
Vancouver, British Columbia
Canada V6M 2H1

People Searching News (Periodical)
P.O. Box 22611
Fort Lauderdale, FL 33335

Post Adoption Center for Education and Research (PACER)
2255 Ygnacio Valley Road, Suite L
Walnut Creek, CA 94598

Post Adoption Centre
Interchange Building, 15 Wilkin Street
London, England NW5 3NG

Triadoption Library
P.O. Box 638
Westminster, CA 92684

REFERENCES

Adams, B. N. (1968). *Kinship in an urban setting.* Chicago: Markham.
Adelberg, R. (1986). A comparison study of searching and non-searching adult adoptees (Doctoral dissertation, Boston University). *Dissertation Abstracts International, 4612B.* (University Microfilms No. 86-02754)
Alexy, W. D. (1982). Dimensions of psychological counseling that facilitate the grieving process of bereaved parents. *Journal of Counseling Psychology, 29,* 498-507.
American Adoption Congress (1990). *Suggested questions and answers about open adoption records.* Washington, DC: Author.
Andersen, R. S. (1989). The nature of adoptee search: Adventure, cure, or growth? *Child Welfare, 68*(6), 623-632.
Anderson, C. (1987). *The birthparents' perspective on adoption.* Des Moines: Concerned United Birthparents.
Arms, S. (1990). *Adoption: A handful of hope.* Berkeley: Celestial Arts.
Attenborough, D. (1990). *The trials of life: A natural history of animal behavior.* Boston: Little, Brown and Company.
Aumend, S., & Barrett, M. (1984). Self-concept and attitudes toward adoption: A comparison of searching and non-searching adult adoptees. *Child Welfare, 63,* 251-259.
Aziz, R. (1990). *C. G. Jung's psychology of religion and synchronicity.* Albany, NY: State University of New York Press.
Baran, A., & Pannor, R. (1988). *Lethal secrets.* CA: Warner Publications.
Baran, A., & Pannor, R. (1990). A time for sweeping change. *Decree, 7*(1), 5.
Baran, A., & Pannor, R. (1990). Open adoption. In D. M. Brodzinsky & M. D. Schechter (Eds.), *The psychology of adoption.* New York and Oxford: Oxford University Press.
Bateson, G. (1988). *Mind and nature: A necessary unity.* New York: Bantam.
Benner, D. G. (1988). *Psychotherapy and the spiritual quest.* Grand Rapids: Baker.
Bernard, H. R., & Killworth, P. D. (1979). A review of small world literature. *Sociological Symposium, 28,* 87-100.
Bernstein, R. (1963). Are we still stereotyping the unmarried mother? In R. Roberts (Ed.), *The unwed mother.* New York: Harper and Row.
Bertocci, D., & Schechter, M. D. (1987). *Adopted adults' perception of their need to search: An informal survey.* Unpublished study.
Bohm, D. (1980). *Wholeness and the implicate order.* London: Routledge and Kegan Paul.
Bohm, D., & Peat, F. D. (1987). *Science, order, and creativity.* New York: Bantam.
Bouchard, T. J., Jr. (1984). Twins reared together and apart: What they tell us about human diversity. In S. W. Fox (Ed.), *The chemical and biological bases of individuality* (pp. 147-178). New York: Plenum.
Bouchard, T. J., Jr., Lykken, D. T., McGue, M., Segal, N. L., & Tellegen, A. (1990, Oct. 12). Sources of human psychological differences: The Minnesota Study of Twins Reared Apart. *Science, 250,* 223-228.
Bowen, M. (1978). *Family therapy in clinical practice.* New York: Jason Aronson.

Bowlby, J. (1958). The nature of the child's tie to his mother. *International Journal of Psycho-Analysis, 39*, 350-373.
Bowlby, J. (1973). *Attachment and loss: Vol. 2. Separation: Anxiety and anger.* London: Hogarth Press and the Institute of Psycho-Analysis.
Bowlby, J. (1980). *Attachment and loss: Vol. 3. Loss, sadness and depression.* New York: Basic Books.
Bozett, F. W. (1985). Male development and fathering throughout the life cycle. *American Behavioral Scientist, 29*, 41-54.
Branton, M., & Snider, E. (Producers). (1990). *The right to know: America's adoption crisis* [Videotape]. Tujunga, CA: Two Peas Productions.
Brinich, P. M. (1980). Some potential effects of adoption on self and object representation. *Psychoanalytic Study of the Child, 35*, 107-133.
Brinich, P. M. (1990). Adoption from the inside out: A psychoanalytic perspective. In D. M. Brodzinsky & M. D. Schechter (Eds.), *The psychology of adoption.* New York and Oxford: Oxford University Press.
Brinich, P. M., Bouchard, T. J., Jr., Speirs, C., & Brown, D. W. (Eds.). (1990). *The adoption bibliography* (2nd ed.). Washington, DC: American Adoption Congress.
Brodzinsky, A. B. (1990). Surrendering an infant for adoption: The birthmother experience. In D. M. Brodzinsky & M. D. Schechter (Eds.), *The psychology of adoption.* New York and Oxford: Oxford University Press.
Brodzinsky, D. M. (1984). New perspectives on adoption revelation. *Adoption and Fostering, 8*, 27-32.
Brodzinsky, D. M. (1987). Adjustment to adoption: A psychosocial perspective. *Clinical Psychology Review, 7*, 25-47.
Brodzinsky, D. M. (1990). A stress and coping model of adoption adjustment. In D. M. Brodzinsky & M. D. Schechter (Eds.), *The psychology of adoption.* New York and Oxford: Oxford University Press.
Brodzinsky, D. M., Schechter, D. E., & Brodzinsky, A. B. (1986). Children's knowledge of adoption: Developmental changes and implications for adjustment. In R. Ashmore & D. M. Brodzinsky (Eds.), *Thinking about the family: Views of parents and children.* Hillsdale, NJ: Lawrence Erlbaum.
Brodzinsky, D. M., & Schechter, M. D. (Eds.). (1990). *The psychology of adoption.* New York and Oxford: Oxford University Press.
Brodzinsky, D. M., Singer, L. M., & Braff, A. M. (1984). Children's understanding of adoption. *Child Development, 55*, 869-878.
Brown, A., Bransford, J., Ferrara, R., & Campione, J. (1983). Learning, remembering and understanding. In P. Mussen (Ed.), *Handbook of child psychology: Vol. 3. Cognitive development.* New York: Wiley.
Brown, F., Driver, S. R., & Briggs, C. A. (Eds.). (1979). *A Hebrew and English lexicon of the Old Testament.* Oxford: Oxford University Press.
Buchheimer, A. (1987). Memory: Preverbal and verbal. In T. R. Verny (Ed.), *Pre- and perinatal psychology: An introduction.* New York: Human Sciences Press.
Burgess, L. C. (1981). *The art of adoption.* New York: Norton.
Burgess, L. C. (1989). *Adoption: How it works.* Cambridge, MA: Burgess Books.
Butterfield, K., & Scaturo, J. (1989, April). *Clinical work with birth families.* Workshop conducted at the meeting of the American Adoption Congress, New York.
Caban v. Mohammed, 99 S.Ct. 1760 (1979).
Cantwell, D. (1975). Genetics of hyperactivity. *Journal of Child Psychology and Psychiatry and Allied Disciplines, 16*, 261-264.

References

Cavalli-Sforza, L. L. (1975). Quantitative genetic perspectives: Implications for human development. In K. W. Schaie, V. E. Anderson, G. E. McClearn, & J. Money (Eds.), *Developmental human behavior genetics.* Lexington, MA: Lexington Books.

Chamberlain, D. (1988). *Babies remember their birth: Extraordinary discoveries about the mind and personality of the newborn.* Los Angeles: Tarcher.

Chapman, C., Dorner, P., Silber, K., & Winterberg, T. S. (1986). Meeting the needs of the adoption triangle through open adoption: The birthmother. *Child and Adolescent Social Work, 3*(4), 203-213.

Chapman, C., Dorner, P., Silber, K., & Winterberg, T. S. (1987). Meeting the needs of the adoption triangle through open adoption: The adoptee. *Child and Adolescent Social Work, 4*(2), 78-91.

Cheek, D. (1986). Prenatal and perinatal imprints: Apparent prenatal consciousness as revealed by hypnosis. *Pre- and Perinatal Psychology Journal, 1*(2), 109.

Child Welfare League of America. (1960). *Standards for services to unmarried parents.* New York: Author.

Child Welfare League of America. (1988). *Standards for services for pregnant adolescents and young parents* (rev. ed.). Washington, DC: Author.

Cicirelli, V. G. (1980). A comparison of college women's feelings toward their siblings and parents. *Journal of Marriage and the Family, 42,* 111-118.

Cissel, B. (1991, March). On long-term rejection. *CUB Communicator,* pp. 12-13. Des Moines: Concerned United Birthparents.

Clothier, F. (1943). Psychological implications of unmarried parenthood. *American Journal of Orthopsychiatry, 13,* 531-549.

Combs, A., & Holland, M. (1990). *Synchronicity: Science, myth, and the trickster.* New York: Paragon House.

Coon, H., Carey, G., & Fulker, D. W. (1990). A simple method of model fitting for adoption data. *Behavior Genetics, 20*(3), 385-404.

DeCasper, A. J. (1985, Feb. 4). Human fetuses perceive maternal speech. *Behavior Today Newsletter, 165*(5), 1-7.

DeCasper, A. J., & Fifer, W. P. (1980, June 6). Of human bonding: Newborns prefer their mothers' voices. *Science, 208,* 1174-1176.

deShazer, S. (1985). *Keys to solution in brief therapy.* New York: Norton.

deShazer, S., Berg, I., Lipchick, E., Nunnally, E., Molnar, A., Gingrich, W., & Weiner-Davis, M. (1986). Brief therapy: Focused solution development. *Family Process, 25,* 207-221.

Deutsch, D. K., Swanson, J. M., Bruell, J. H., Cantwell, D. P., Weinberg, F., & Baren, M. (1982). Overrepresentation of adoptees in children with the attention deficit disorder. *Behavior Genetics, 12,* 231-238.

Deykin, E., Campbell, L., & Patti, P. (1984). The post-adoption experience of surrendering parents. *American Journal of Orthopsychiatry, 54,* 271-280.

Deykin, E., Patti, P., & Ryan, J. (1988). Fathers of adopted children: A study of the impact of child surrender on birthfathers. *American Journal of Orthopsychiatry, 58*(2), 240-248.

Diaconis, P., & Mosteller, F. (1989). Methods for studying coincidences. *Journal of the American Statistical Association, 84*(408), 853-861.

Dudrear, B. U. (1991). *The female hero's journey toward wholeness: Psychospiritual aspects of birthmothers who searched and reunited with children relinquished for adoption.* Doctoral dissertation, University for Humanistic Studies, Del Mar, CA.

Earnshaw, A. (1987). Temporal transmission of parental life events to children. In T. R. Verny (Ed.), *Pre- and perinatal psychology: An introduction* (pp. 219-233). New York: Human Sciences Press.

Earnshaw, A. (1990). Autism as a family affair. *Australian Journal of Psychotherapy, 9*(1), 46-61.
Eason, C. (1990). *The psychic power of children.* London: Rider.
Eaves, L. J., Eysenck, H. J., & Martin, N. G. (1989). *Genes, culture and personality: An empirical approach.* London: Academic Press.
Edinger, E. (1987). *The Christian archetype.* Toronto: Inner City Books.
Ehrenwald, J. (1977). Psi phenomena and brain research. In B. B. Wolman (Ed.), *Handbook of parapsychology* (pp. 716-727). New York: Van Nostrand Reinhold.
Eliot, T. S. (1963). *Collected poems 1909-1962.* New York: Harcourt, Brace and World.
Erikson, E. (1963). *Childhood and society* (2nd ed.). New York: Norton.
Erikson, E. (1968). *Identity: Youth and crisis.* New York: Norton.
Falk, R. (1975). *The perception of randomness.* Doctoral dissertation (in Hebrew), The Hebrew University, Jerusalem.
Falk, R. (1982). On coincidences. *Skeptical Inquirer, 6*(2), 18-31.
Falk, R., & MacGregor, D. (1983). The surprisingness of coincidences. In P. Humphreys, O. Svenson, & A. Vari (Eds.), *Analysing and aiding decision processes* (pp. 489-502). New York: North-Holland.
Farrant, G. (1987). Cellular consciousness. *Aesthema, 7*, 28-39. Keynote address at the 14th International Primal Association Convention, 1986, with interview by A. Buchheimer, 40-45.
Feder, L. (1980). Preconceptive ambivalence and internal reality. *International Journal of Psychoanalysis, 61*(2), 161-178.
Fonda, A. B. (1984). Birthmothers who search: An exploratory study (Doctoral dissertation, California School of Professional Psychology, Berkeley). *Dissertation Abstracts International,* 4502B. (University Microfilms No. 84-11248)
Freud, S. (1934). Dreams and the occult. In *New introductory lectures on psychoanalysis.* London: Hogarth Press.
Freud, S. (1955). Beyond the pleasure principle. In J. Strachey (Ed. and Trans.), *The standard edition of the complete psychological works of Sigmund Freud* (Vol. 18). London: Hogarth Press. (Original work published 1920)
Freud, S. (1957). Mourning and melancholia. In J. Strachey (Ed. and Trans.), *The standard edition of the complete psychological works of Sigmund Freud* (Vol. 14). London: Hogarth Press. (Original work published 1917)
Freud, S. (1963). *Studies in parapsychology: The uncanny: Dreams and telepathy: A neurosis of demonical possession.* New York: Collier.
Friedman, I. (Trans. and Commentator). (1977). *Sefer yezirah* [The book of creation]. New York: S. Weiser.
Frisk, M. (1964). Identity problems and confused conceptions of the genetic ego in adopted children during adolescence. *Acta Paedo Psychiatrica, 31*, 6-12.
Fromm, E. (1956). *The art of loving.* New York: Harper and Row.
Galton, F. (1875). The history of twins as a criterion of the relative powers of nature and nurture. *Journal of the Anthropological Institute, 6*, 391-406.
Ganz, S. (1987). *pretend it didnt happen* [sic] [Drama]. San Francisco: Author.
Gatlin, L. L. (1977). Meaningful information creation: An alternative interpretation of the psi phenomenon. *Journal of the American Society for Psychical Research, 71*, 1-17.
Gediman, J. S., & Brown, L. P. (1989). *BirthBond: Reunions between birthparents and adoptees--what happens after.* Far Hills, NJ: New Horizon Press.
Gehring, W. J. (1985). The homeo box: A key to understanding of development? *Cell, 40*, 3-5.

References

Gelman, R., & Baillargeon, R. (1983). A review of some Piagetian concepts. In P. Mussen (Ed.), *Handbook of child psychology: Vol. 3: Cognitive development.* New York: Wiley.

Gilligan, S. G. (1987). *Therapeutic trances: The cooperation principle in Ericksonian hypnotherapy.* New York: Brunner/Mazel.

Gispen, W. H., Perumal, R., Wilson, J. E., & Glassman, E. (1977). Phosphorylation of proteins of synaptosome-enriched fractions of brain during short-term training experience: The effects of various behavioral treatments. *Behavioral Biology, 21*(3), 358-363.

Goodman, J., Silberstein, M. R., & Mandel, W. (1963). Adopted children brought to psychiatric clinics. *Archives of General Psychiatry, 9*, 451-456.

Goodrich, W., Fullerton, C. S., Yates, B. T., & Berman, L. B. (1990). The residential treatment of severely disturbed adolescent adoptees. In D. M. Brodzinsky & M. D. Schechter (Eds.), *The psychology of adoption.* New York and Oxford: Oxford University Press.

Gribbin, J. (1984). *In search of Schrödinger's cat: Quantum physics and reality.* New York: Bantam.

Griffith, K. C. (Ed.). (1991). *The right to know who you are: Reform of adoption law with honesty, openness and integrity.* Ottawa: Katherine Kimbell.

Grof, S. (1985). *Beyond the brain: Birth, death, and transcendence in psychotherapy.* Albany: State University of New York Press.

Grotevant, H. D., & McRoy, R. G. (1990). Adopted adolescents in residential treatment: The role of the family. In D. M. Brodzinsky & M. D. Schechter (Eds.), *The psychology of adoption.* New York and Oxford: Oxford University Press.

Haley, A. (1976). *Roots: The saga of an American family.* New York: Doubleday.

Hardy, A., Harvie, R., & Koestler, A. (1973). *The challenge of chance.* New York: Random House.

Havens, L. (1989, April). *The psychological possession of human beings: De-infantilizing adoption.* Workshop conducted at the meeting of the American Adoption Congress, New York.

Hawking, S., & Penrose, R. (1970). The singularities of gravitational collapse and cosmology. *Proceedings of the Royal Society of London, A314*, 529-548.

Herskowitz, I., Blair, L., Forbes, D., Hicks, J., Kassir, Y., Kushner, P., Rine, J., Sprague, G., & Strathern, J. (1980). Control of cell type in the yeast *Saccharomyces cerevisiae* and a hypothesis for development in higher eukaryotes. In T. Leighton & W. F. Loomis (Eds.), *The molecular genetics of development* (pp. 79-118). New York: Academic Press.

Holden, C. (1980, March 21). Identical twins reared apart. *Science, 207*, 1323-1327.

Horney, K. (1945). *Our inner conflicts: A constructive theory of neurosis.* New York: Norton.

Iwanek, M. (1990, May). *We opened records in New Zealand.* Workshop conducted at the meeting of the American Adoption Congress, Chicago.

Jackson, D. D. (1980, October). Reunion of identical twins, raised apart, reveals some astonishing similarities. *Smithsonian*, pp. 48-56.

James, W. (1920). *A pluralistic universe.* New York: Longmans Green.

James, W. (1961). *The varieties of religious experience.* New York: Macmillan.

Jensen, G.D., & Tolman, C. W. (1962). Mother-infant relationship in the monkey, *Macaca nemestrina*: The effect of brief separation and mother-infant specificity. *Journal of Comparative Physiology and Psychology, 55*, 131-136.

Jernberg, A. M. (1989). Attachment enhancing for adopted children. In P. V. Grabe (Ed.), *Adoption resources for mental health professionals.* New Brunswick, NJ: Rutgers University, Transaction Publishers.

Judson, H. F. (1979). *The eighth day of creation.* New York: Touchstone Books, Simon and Schuster.
Jung, C. G. (1958). *Psychology and religion: West and East.* New York: Pantheon.
Jung, C. G. (1960). *The structure and dynamics of the psyche. Collected works* (Vol. 8). London: Routledge and Kegan Paul.
Jung, C. G. (1971). *Psychological types. Collected works* (Vol. 6). Princeton, NJ: Princeton University Press.
Jung, C. G., & Pauli, W. (1955). *The interpretation of nature and the psyche.* New York: Pantheon. (Original work published 1952)
Kadushin, A. (1974). *Child welfare services.* New York: Macmillan.
Kadushin, A. (1980). *Child welfare services* (3rd ed.). New York: Macmillan.
Kamin, L. (1981). Studies of adopted children. In H. J. Eysenck & L. Kamin (Eds.), *The intelligence controversy.* New York: Wiley-Interscience.
Kammerer, P. (1919). *Das gesetz der serie: Eine lehre von den wiederholungen im lebens--und im weltgeschehen* [The law of seriality: A doctrine of repetitions in events in life and society]. Stuttgart and Berlin: Deutsche Verlags-Anstalt.
Kammerer, P. (1924). *The inheritance of acquired characteristics* (A. P. Maerker-Branden, Trans.). New York: Boni and Liveright.
Kaplan, S. (1989, April). *Sexuality and adoption.* Workshop conducted at the meeting of the American Adoption Congress, New York.
Khamsi, S. (1987). Birth feelings: A phenomenological investigation. *Aesthema, 7,* 46-60.
Kierkegaard, S. (1941). *The sickness unto death.* Princeton, NJ: Princeton University Press.
Kirk, H. D. (1964). *Shared fate: A theory of adoption and mental health.* New York: Free Press.
Kirk, H. D. (1985). *Adoptive kinship: A modern institution in need of reform.* Port Angeles, WA: Ben Simon.
Kirk, H. D., Jonassohn, K., & Fisch, A. (1966). Are adopted children especially vulnerable to stress? *Archives of General Psychiatry, 14,* 291-298.
Kirschner, D. (1987, May). *The adopted child syndrome.* Paper presented at the meeting of the American Adoption Congress, Boston.
Kirschner, D., & Nagel, L. S. (1988). Antisocial behavior in adoptees: Patterns and dynamics. *Child and Adolescent Social Work, 5*(4), 300-314.
Kirschvink, J. L., Kobayashi-Kirschvink, A., & Woodford, B. J. (in press). Magnetite biomineralization in the human brain. *Proceedings of the National Academy of Sciences.*
Koestler, A. (1971). *The case of the midwife toad.* New York: Random House.
Koestler, A. (1972). *The roots of coincidence.* New York: Random House.
Krippner, S. (Ed.) (1978). *Extrasensory perception.* New York: Plenum.
Lazare, A. (1979). Unresolved grief. In A. Lazare (Ed.), *Outpatient psychiatry: Diagnosis and treatment.* Baltimore: Williams and Wilkins.
Lee, T. R., Mancini, J. A., & Maxwell, J. W. (1990). Sibling relationships in adulthood: Contact patterns and motivations. *Journal of Marriage and the Family, 52,* 431-440.
Lehr v. Robertson, 103 S.Ct. 2985 (1983).
Lewontin, R. C. (1975). Genetic aspects of intelligence. *Annual Review of Genetics, 9,* 387-405.
Lifton, B. J. (1988). *Lost and found: The adoption experience.* New York: Harper and Row.
Lifton, B. J. (1992). *The adopted self: Towards a theory of cumulative trauma.* Doctoral thesis, Union Institute, Cincinnati.
Lifton, R. J. (1976). On the adoption experience. Foreword to M. K. Benet, *The politics of adoption* (pp. 1-7). New York: Free Press.
Lifton, R. J. (1979). *The broken connection.* New York: Simon and Schuster.

References

Lindemann, E. (1944). Symptomatology and the management of acute grief. *American Journal of Psychiatry, 101*, 141-148.

Lumsden, C. J., & Wilson, E. O. (1981). *Genes, mind and culture.* Cambridge, MA: Harvard University Press.

Lykken, D. T., McGue, M., Bouchard, T. J., Jr., & Tellegen, A. (1990). Does contact lead to similarity or similarity to contact? *Behavior Genetics, 20*(5), 547-562.

Marlin, E. (1989). *Genograms: The new tool for exploring the personality, career, and love patterns you inherit.* Chicago: Contemporary Books.

Marquis, K. S., & Detweiler, R. A. (1985). Does adoption mean different? An attributional analysis. *Journal of Personality and Social Psychology, 48*, 1054-1066.

Martino, G. (1989, April). *Search: A developmental milestone.* Workshop conducted at the meeting of the American Adoption Congress, New York.

Maslow, A. (1964). *Religions, values, and peak experiences.* Columbus: Ohio State University Press.

May, R. (1975). *The courage to create.* New York: Norton.

McGoldrick, M., & Gerson, R. (1985). *Genograms in family assessment.* New York: Norton.

McKenna, J. J. (1987). An anthropological perspective on the sudden infant death syndrome: A testable hypothesis on the possible role of parental breathing cues in promoting infant breathing stability, part 1. *Pre- and Perinatal Psychology Journal, 2*(2), 93-135. [A modified version of an article in (1986) *Medical anthropology: Cross-cultural studies in disease and illness, 10*(1)].

McRoy, R. G., Grotevant, H. D., & White, K. L. (1988). *Openness in adoption: New practices, new issues.* New York: Praeger.

Meerloo, J. A. (1964). *Hidden communion: Studies in the communication theory of telepathy.* New York: Garrett.

Menlove, F. L. (1965). Aggressive symptoms in emotionally disturbed adopted children. *Child Development, 36*, 519-532.

Midford, S. (1986). *The development of a model and measure of adoptee identity.* Unpublished master's dissertation, University of Tasmania, Australia.

Midford, S. (1987). A measure of adoptee identity. *Uniview, 6*(1), 8-9.

Millen, L., & Roll, S. (1985, July). Solomon's mothers: A special case of pathological bereavement. *American Journal of Orthopsychiatry, 55*(3), 411-418.

Millen, L., Roll, S., & Backlund, B. (1986). Solomon's mothers: Mourning in mothers who relinquish their children for adoption. In T. A. Rando (Ed.), *Parental loss of a child* (pp. 257-268). Champaign, IL: Research Press.

Miller, J. G. (1978). *Living systems.* New York: McGraw-Hill.

Miller-Havens, S. (1990). Connections and disconnections: birth origin fantasies of adopted women who search (Doctoral dissertation, Harvard University). *Dissertation Abstracts International,* 5103B. (University Microfilms No. 90-21130)

Möbius, A. F. (1865). *Königlich sächsischen ges. der wiss. zu Leipzig, 17,* 3I-68 = *Werke, 2,* 473-512.

Modell, J. (1986). In search: The purported biological basis of parenthood. *American Ethnologist, 13,* 646-661.

Moore, K. A., & Burt, M. R. (1982). *Private crisis, public costs: Policy perspectives on teenage childbearing.* Washington, DC: Urban Institute Press.

Murphy, L. B. (Ed.) (1989). *There is more beyond: Selected papers of Gardner Murphy.* Jefferson, NC: McFarland.

Musser, S. K. (1982). *What kind of love is this? A story of adoption reconciliation.* Cape Coral, FL: Jan Publications.

Nave, L. R. (1989). *Christian counseling practices and the American adoption system.* Unpublished manuscript. Rocky River, OH.

Neumann, E. (1973, 1990). *The child.* New York: G. P. Putnam; Boston: Shambhala.

Nickman, S. L. (1985). Losses in adoption: The need for dialogue. *Psychoanalytic study of the child, 40,* 365-398.

NIV Study Bible (New International Version). (1985). Grand Rapids, MI: Zondervan. NIV text (1984). East Brunswick, NJ: International Bible Society.

Offord, D. R., Aponte, J. F., & Cross, L. A. (1969). Presenting symptomatology of adopted children. *Archives of General Psychiatry, 20,* 110-116.

O'Hanlon, W. (1987). *Taproots.* New York: Norton.

O'Leary, K. M., Shore, M. F., & Wilder, S. (1984). Contacting pregnant adolescents: Are we missing cues? *Social Casework, 65,* 297-305.

Otto, R. (1958). *The idea of the holy.* New York and Oxford: Oxford University Press.

Oxford English Dictionary (Vol. 3). (1989). Oxford: Clarendon Press.

Paigen, K. (1980). Temporal genes and other developmental regulators in mammals. In T. Leighton and W. F. Loomis (Eds.), *The molecular genetics of development* (pp. 419-470). New York: Academic Press.

Panneton, R. K. (1985). Prenatal auditory experience with melodies: Effects on postnatal auditory preferences in human newborns (Doctoral dissertation, University of North Carolina, Greensboro). *Dissertation Abstracts International,* 4709B. (University Microfilms No. 87-01335)

Pannor, R., Baran, A., & Sorosky, A. (1978). Birthparents who relinquished babies for adoption revisited. *Family Process, 17,* 329-337.

Pannor, R., Sorosky, A., & Baran, A. (1974). Opening the sealed record in adoption: The human need for continuity. *Journal of Jewish Communal Service, 51,* 188-196.

Parkes, C. M. (1972). *Bereavement: Studies of grief in adult life.* New York: International Universities Press.

Pascal, B. (1958). *Pascal's pensées.* New York: E. P. Dutton. (Original work published 1660)

Pavao, J. M. (1989, April). *Post-search issues.* Workshop conducted at the meeting of the American Adoption Congress, New York.

Peat, F. D. (1987). *Synchronicity: The bridge between matter and mind.* New York: Bantam.

Peck, M. S. (1978). *The road less traveled.* New York: Simon and Schuster.

Penrose, R. (1989). *The emperor's new mind: Concerning computers, minds, and the laws of physics.* Oxford: Oxford University Press.

Piaget, J. (1930). *The child's conception of physical causality.* London: Kegan Paul.

Plomin, R. (1986). *Development, genetics, and psychology.* Hillsdale, NJ: Lawrence Erlbaum.

Plomin, R., & Daniels, D. (1987). Why are children in the same family so different from one another? *Behavioral and Brain Sciences, 10,* 1-16.

Plomin, R., & DeFries, J. C. (1985). *Origins of individual differences in infancy. The Colorado Adoption Project.* Orlando, FL: Academic Press.

Plomin, R., Defries, J. C., & Roberts, M. K. (1977). Assortive mating by unwed biological parents of adopted children. *Science, 196,* 449-450.

Pribram, K. (1984). The holographic hypothesis of brain function: A meeting of minds. In S. Grof (Ed.), *Ancient wisdom and modern science.* Albany: State University of New York Press.

Pribram, K. H., & Broadbent, D. E. (1970). *Biology of memory.* New York: Academic Press.

Profiles: Search and reunion. (1989, February). *People Searching News, 2*(5), 24.

Przibram, H. (1926, November). Paul Kammerer als biologe, *Monistische Monatshefte.*

Quilloin v. Walcott, 98 S.Ct. 549 (1978).

Rando, T. A. (Ed.). (1986). *Parental loss of a child.* Champaign, IL: Research Press.
Raphael, B. (1983). *The anatomy of bereavement.* New York: Basic Books.
Raynor, L. (1980). *The adopted child comes of age.* London: George Allen and Unwin.
Reed, G. (1988). *The psychology of anomalous experience: A cognitive approach.* Buffalo, NY: Prometheus Books.
Reeves, A. C. (1971). Children with surrogate parents: Cases seen in analytic therapy and an aetiological hypothesis. *British Journal of Medical Psychology, 44,* 155-171.
Reiss, P. J. (1962). The extended kinship system: Correlates of and attitudes on frequency of interaction. *Marriage and Family Living, 24,* 333-339.
Reynolds, W. F., Eisnitz, M. F., Chiappise, D., & Walsh, M. (1976, August). *Personality factors differentiating searching and non-searching adoptees.* Paper presented at the annual convention of the American Psychological Association, Washington, DC.
Rhine, L. E. (1967). *ESP in life and lab: Tracing hidden channels.* New York: Macmillan.
Riben, M. (1988). *Shedding light on the dark side of adoption.* Detroit: Harlo.
Rillera, M. J. (1987). *Adoption encounter: Hurt, transition, healing.* Westminster, CA: Triadoption Publications.
Rillera, M. J. (1991). *The reunion book: Vol. I.* Westminster, CA: Triadoption Publications.
Ring, K. (1984). *Heading toward omega.* New York: William Morrow.
Roberts, R. M. (1989). *Serendipity: Accidental discoveries in science.* New York: John Wiley and Sons.
Rogers, R. (1969). The adolescent and the hidden parent. *Comprehensive Psychiatry, 10,* 296-301.
Rose, R. J., & Ditto, W. B. (1983). A developmental-genetic analysis of common fears from early adolescence to early adulthood. *Child Development, 54,* 361-368.
Rose, R. J., & Kaprio, J. (1988). Frequency of social contact and intrapair resemblance of adult monozygotic cotwins: Or does shared experience influence personality after all? *Behavior Genetics, 18,* 309-328.
Rosen, C. M. (1987, September). The eerie world of reunited twins. *Discover,* pp. 36-46.
Rosen, D. (1973). Suicide survivors: A follow-up study of persons who survived jumping from the Golden Gate and San Francisco-Oakland Bay Bridges. *Western Journal of Medicine, 122,* 289.
Rotundo, E. A. (1985). American fatherhood: A historical perspective. *American Behavioral Scientist, 29,* 7-24.
Rynearson, E. K. (1982). Relinquishment and its maternal complications: A preliminary study. *American Journal of Psychiatry, 139*(3), 338-340.
Sachdev, P. (1989). The triangle of fears: Fallacies and facts. *Child Welfare, 68*(5), 491-503.
Sants, H. J. (1964). Genealogical bewilderment in children with substitute parents. *British Journal of Medical Psychology, 37,* 133-141.
Schaefer, C. (1991). *The other mother: A woman's love for the child she gave up for adoption.* New York: Soho Press.
Schaeffer, F. A. (1968). *The God who is there: Speaking historic Christianity into the twentieth century.* Downers Grove, IL: Inter-Varsity Press.
Schaffer, J., & Lindstrom, C. (1990). Brief solution-focused therapy with adoptive families. In D. M. Brodzinsky & M. D. Schechter (Eds.), *The psychology of adoption.* New York and Oxford: Oxford University Press.
Schechter, M., Carlson, P. V., Simmons, J. Q., & Work, H. H. (1964). Emotional problems in the adoptee. *Archives of General Psychiatry, 10,* 37-46.
Schneider, J. (1984). *Stress, loss and grief.* Baltimore: University Park Press.
Schopenhauer, A. (1891). Parerga und paralipomena. E. Griesbach (Ed.), *Samtliche Werke,* Vol. 4. Leipzig: Philipp Reclam.

Schumacher, J. D. (1984). Helping children cope with a sibling's death. In J. C. Hansen (Ed.), *Death and grief in the family*. Rockville, MD: Aspen Systems.

Schwarz, B. E. (1971). *Parent-child telepathy: A study of the telepathy of everyday life*. New York: Garrett.

Schwarz, B. E. (1975). Telepathic humoresque. *Psychoanalytic Review, 61*(4), 591-606.

Schwarz, B. E. (1980). *Psychic-nexus: Psychic phenomena in psychiatry and everyday life*. New York: Van Nostrand Reinhold.

Segal, N. L., Grove, W. M., & Bouchard, T. J., Jr. (in press). Psychiatric investigations and findings from the Minnesota Study of Twins Reared Apart. In M. Tsuang, K. Kendler, & M. Lyons (Eds.), *Genetic issues in psychiatric epidemiology*. New Brunswick, NJ: Rutgers University Press.

Shallis, M. (1983). *On time: An investigation into scientific knowledge and human experience*. New York: Schocken.

Sheldrake, R. (1981). *A new science of life*. Los Angeles: Tarcher.

Silverman, P. R. (1981). *Helping women cope with grief*. Beverly Hills, CA: Sage Publications.

Silverman, P. R., Campbell, L., Patti, P., & Style, C. B. (1988). Reunions between adoptees and birth parents: The birth parents' experience. *Social Work, 33*(6), 523-528.

Silverman, P. R., & Patti, P. (1989, April). *The impact of reunions*. Workshop conducted at the meeting of the American Adoption Congress, New York.

Simon, N. M., & Senturia, A. G. (1966). Adoption and psychiatric illness. *American Journal of Psychiatry, 122*, 858-867.

Singer, L. M., Brodzinsky, D. M., & Braff, A. M. (1982). Children's belief about adoption: A developmental study. *Journal of Applied Developmental Psychology, 3*, 285-294.

Slater, Ronda. (1984). *"...a name you never got"* [sic] [Drama]. Oakland, CA: Baby Bunny Productions.

Small, J. W. (1987). Working with adoptive families. *Public Welfare, 45*, 33-41.

Sobol, M., & Cardiff, J. (1983). A sociopsychological investigation of adult adoptees' search for birth parents. *Family Relations, 32*, 477-483.

Sorich, C. J., & Siebert, R. (1982). Toward humanizing adoption. *Child Welfare, 61*, 207-213.

Sorosky, A., Baran, A., & Pannor, R. (1975). Identity conflicts in adoptees. *American Journal of Orthopsychiatry, 45*, 18-27.

Sorosky, A., Baran, A., & Pannor, R. (1978, 1989). *The adoption triangle: Sealed or open records: How they affect adoptees, birth parents, and adoptive parents*. San Antonio, TX: Corona.

Stanley v. Illinois, 92 S.Ct. 1208 (1972).

Stephenson, J. (1986). Grief of siblings. In T. A. Rando (Ed.), *Parental loss of a child*. Champaign, IL: Research Press.

Stevens, A. (1982). *Archetypes: A natural history of the self*. New York: William Morrow.

Stiffler, L. H. (1991). Adoption's impact on birthmothers: "Can a mother forget her child?" *Journal of Psychology and Christianity, 10*(3), 249-259.

Stiffler, L. H. (1991). *Parent-child synchronicities during years of separation by adoption: Anomalous connecting information in histories of union/loss/reunion*. Doctoral dissertation, Oxford Graduate School, Dayton, TN. (University Microfilms No. LD-02254)

Stiffler, L. H. (in press). Adoptees and birthparents connected by design: Surprising synchronicities in histories of union/loss/reunion. *Pre- and Perinatal Psychology Journal*.

Stone, F. H. (1972). Adoption and identity. *Child Psychiatry and Human Development, 2*, 120-128.

References

Tellegen, A., Lykken, D. T., Bouchard, T. J., Jr., Wilcox, K. J., Segal, N. L., & Rich, S. (1988). Personality similarity in twins reared apart and together. *Journal of Personality and Social Psychology, 54*(6), 1031-1039.

Thompson, J., Stoneman, L., Webber, J., & Harrison, D. (1978). *The adoption rectangle: A study of adult adoptees' search for birth family history and implications for adoption service.* Unpublished project report, Children's Aid Society of Metropolitan Toronto.

Triseliotis, J. (1973). *In search of origins: The experiences of adopted people.* London: Routledge and Kegan Paul.

Van Why, E. (1977). *Adoption bibliography and multi-ethnic sourcebook.* Hartford: Open Door Society of Connecticut.

Verny, T. R. (Ed.). (1987). *Pre- and perinatal psychology: An introduction.* New York: Human Sciences Press.

Verny, T. R., & Kelly, J. (1981). *The secret life of the unborn child.* New York: Summit Books.

Verrier, N. (1987). The primal wound: A preliminary investigation into the effects of separation from the birth mother on adopted children. *Pre- and Perinatal Psychology Journal, 2*(2), 75-86.

Volkan, V. D. (1984-1985). Complicated mourning. *Annals of Psychoanalysis, 12-13,* 323-348.

Walters, L. H., & Elam, A. W. (1985). The father and the law. *American Behavioral Scientist, 29,* 78-111.

Winnicott, D. W. (1956). Primary maternal preoccupation. In D. W. Winnicott, *Collected papers.* London: Tavistock.

Winkler, R. C., & van Keppel, M. (1984). *Relinquishing mothers in adoption: Their long-term adjustment* (Monograph No. 3). Melbourne: Institute of Family Studies.

Winkler, R. C., Brown, D. W., van Keppel, M., & Blanchard, A. (1988). *Clinical practice in adoption.* New York and Oxford: Pergamon.

Zill, N. (1985, April). *Behavior and learning problems among adopted children: Findings from a U.S. national survey of child health.* Paper presented at the meeting of the Society for Research in Child Development, Toronto.

Zinkin, L. (1987). The hologram as a model for analytical psychology. *Journal of Analytical Psychology, 32,* 1-21.

Zisook, S., & DeVaul, R. (1985). Unresolved grief. *American Journal of Psychoanalysis, 45,* 370-379.

Zusne, L., & Jones, W. H. (1989). *Anomalistic psychology: A study of magical thinking* (2nd ed.). Hillsdale, NJ: Lawrence Erlbaum.